GET OFF YOUR KNEES

GET OFF

A STORY OF FAITH, COURAGE, AND DETERMINATION

YOUR
KNEES

JOHN ROBINSON

with Dave Allen

Syracuse University Press

First Edition 2009

09   10   11   12   13   14   6   5   4   3   2   1

All photographs courtesy of the author.

∞ The paper used in this publication meets the minimum requirements
of the American National Standard for Information Sciences—Permanence
of Paper for Printed Library Materials, ANSI Z39.48-1992.

For a listing of books published and distributed by Syracuse University Press,
visit our Web site at SyracuseUniversityPress.syr.edu

ISBN: 978-0-8156-0922-3

Library of Congress Cataloging-in-Publication Data

Robinson, John, 1968–

    Get off your knees : a story of faith, courage, and determination / John
Robinson ; with Dave Allen. — 1st ed.

        p. cm.

    ISBN 978-0-8156-0922-3 (cloth : alk. paper)

    1. Robinson, John, 1968–   2. Christian biography—United States.   3. People
with disabilities—Religious life.   4. People with disabilities—United States—
Biography.   I. Allen, Dave, 1968–   II. Title.

    BR1725.R6246A3 2009

    277.3'083092—dc22

        [B]   2009032808

Manufactured in the United States of America

To Andrea, with all my love

JOHN ROBINSON has twenty years of sales experience in media and is a 1990 graduate of the S. I. Newhouse School of Public Communications at Syracuse University. John has been married for more than sixteen years and has three children. In 2001 he was selected to carry the Olympic torch as it passed through Albany on its way to Salt Lake City for the 2002 Winter Olympic Games.

DAVE ALLEN is coauthor of *Golf Annika's Way*, with Annika Sorenstam, and *Golf Rx: A 15-Minute-a-Day Core Program for More Yards*, with Vijay Vad, M.D. He is currently an editor with GolfChannel.com and lives in Orlando, Florida.

CONTENTS

Illustrations

Acknowledgments

MY JOURNEY TO DATE has crossed the lives of many people—family, friends, coworkers. I would not have the strength, courage, and determination to overcome my physical obstacles without the love and support of these people.

First and foremost is my wife, Andrea, who has been my best friend, cheerleader, drill sergeant, and inspiration. The dream of the life we have built over the years has motivated me to be who I am today. My children—Haydon, Ariel, and Owen—continue to provide me the experience and wisdom to take every hurdle with more patience.

My father's friendship, perseverance, love, and guidance built within me the faith that is the very mortar of my interpersonal foundation. The irony is that I don't think he ever set out to impose his will, but by the grace of God that is exactly what he did. Without this pillar of faith, I would not be able to function. I cannot say thank you enough.

In our early years together, my sister, Katherine Mary Robinson, became a friend, companion, and role model. Whether it was driving across the country, swimming in the lake, or just laughing around the house, Katherine could not have been a better sister.

My uncle Douglas is an extremely intelligent, practical, and nurturing individual. He's been part-parent and friend to me, especially at times when I needed someone to advise me or just listen. Daniel Willet provided an appreciation for Syracuse University, intelligent conversation, and counsel on how to be a young man. He has been sorely missed. Jacob Burge Morris, my grandfather, threw tennis balls to me for hours so I could learn to hit a baseball. He would let me ride in the wagon behind his tractor every summer, which, for me, was the most magical thing in the world. There isn't a day that goes by that I don't think about his kind spirit.

In life there are people who love you because they are family or linked to you in some way, and then there are those people who choose to be your friend. Jeff Rupert made more of an impact on me than he will ever know, and more than I will ever be able to repay. Jeff was the first person to be my friend because of who I am as an individual. I've been blessed with twenty-plus years of friendships, thanks to my good fortune to attend Syracuse University. Craig Hubmeier is the brother I never had. We laughed a lot, shared a lot, and secretly enjoyed our table-hockey disagreements. Dave Allen has been a godparent, golf partner, travel companion, and now biographer. Pat Kelleher is who I want to be when I grow up. Paul Golden will give you the shirt off his back. Scott Roegiers has a laugh and spirit that I think about every day. Jivi Govender is someone I feel I've known through many lifetimes, and knew it the first time I met him. Robert Aronow cares about everyone he has met. He has an uncanny ability to read people and a force within him that brings all types together, including us.

Finally, it takes a mother's love (and her mother's love) to put it all into perspective. Helen McVoy Morris (Gram), whether she knows it or not, is the beacon of light. Gram is the best combination of force, determination, and love that I needed to retreat to each summer, in college, and as an adult. My mother, Priscilla Morris Robinson, always told me that we were exactly alike. I am reminded every day of the many drives we took together in the car, when she would hold the end of my arm in her hand, as if we were holding hands. As I grew into adulthood and had children of my own, I began to see that she was right. And as I go through life without my mother, I know that she is with me.

INTRODUCTION

Finding Inspiration in My Story

IT TOOK A GREAT FRIEND to make me realize that I am an inspiration to others. There were many instances in college or early in my sales career when I'd be walking to class or out on a sales call and people would stop me and say, "Hey, that's really great," or "How'd you do that?" I didn't think I was doing anything extraordinary. I was different, but I didn't want to be viewed as someone with a physical disability. I wanted to stand on my own and be seen as the equal of any able-bodied person. I expected to get a degree, to hold down a job, and to be a productive member of society. There was a part of me that didn't want to look at it like, "Maybe I am inspirational. Maybe I can help somebody."

For me, the turning point came in the summer of 2000. I had moved to Albany to take a sales job with NBC affiliate station WNYT, and was staying with a college roommate, Paul Golden, while my family made arrangements to move from Syracuse. One night after work I mentioned to Paul that a client had stopped my presentation that day to tell me what an inspiration I was, and how much that bothered me. Paul said, "Get over it, John!

You are." Then he reminded me of a trip in college when a group of us went to Atlantic City for spring break. We were hanging around the blackjack table in one casino when this older gentleman, who had obviously had too much to drink, practically jumped me to tell me what an inspiration I was and how helpful it would be if I could talk to his wheelchair-bound brother. His fast approach was troublesome to my friends, who thought he was dangerous. But I told them it was fine and spoke to the man and his brother for a few minutes.

Ten years later, Paul reminded me that I needed to act toward my client like I did with those strangers in Atlantic City. He was right, of course. I have come to realize that people who don't see me every day are going to have that kind of reaction toward me, and they might be put off or surprised by how I look. I have to be able to deal with that and either calm them down or address it head-on, as I did in Atlantic City. It takes confidence in knowing I have triumphed over a great deal of adversity, but it also means I have to recognize that yes, I do have the ability to inspire others.

My story on the surface is complex, but basically comes down to being willing to overcome the "obstacles" I have been given in life. I was born a congenital amputee without the extension of my arms and my legs, and as an adult stand three-foot-nine off the floor, or about as tall as most bar stools. I have no hands and fingers to type or hold a fork with, and have adapted to an able-bodied world using what others would consider elbows. I have a successful career and a family and am a relatively independent individual. I can drive a car, walk on a treadmill, coach my son's soccer team, and hit a golf ball more than 150 yards. One rainy day in Ireland I even managed to poke one out there 205 yards!

I've been able to live what many would consider a "normal" life because I viewed these obstacles not as a dead end but rather as opportunities for growth. This is a central theme throughout this book, and one I have lived every day of my life. And it doesn't just apply to people with disabilities. A salesperson can see a high sales goal as an obstacle or can view it as an opportunity to succeed. A student can see a large number of classes as an obstacle, or as an opportunity to advance her knowledge base and become the best she can be. A single parent can see the burden of raising children alone as an obstacle, or as an opportunity to teach them the importance of love and the true bond that exists between parents and their children.

In my life, the greatest obstacle is not knowing how people are going to react to me, especially when they're meeting me for the first time. But I also view this as an opportunity, because as a salesperson you want a prospective client to remember you. If the local Honda dealer remembers me because of how I look, that's to my advantage. The obstacles I've faced have also allowed me to adapt my problem-solving skills faster than most of my competitors. I've had to learn how to dress myself on my own, use a PDA, carry my books from class to class, and ride the subway without getting trampled. What that's done is teach me how to solve a problem relatively quickly, and that's all the sales business really is.

Too often in life we look for an excuse instead of trying to find the real solution to the problem; even the disabled community is guilty of this from time to time. We're quick to blame our troubles on someone or something else, instead of taking responsibility for our situation and taking action to do something about it. After graduating from college, I interviewed with twenty-five television stations in Canada and the United States over a four-year period before one, WSTM in Syracuse, would take a chance on me. It took me three interviews to convince them I was right for the job—it helped that I accepted their 100 percent commission offer—but I knew I had a skill to offer them, and I wasn't going to stop until I convinced them.

What it really boils down to is one word—*responsibility*! We are all looking for an excuse as a way out of the problems we confront and are not challenged to look at ourselves objectively. One of the things I believe my disability has done for me is provide me with the ability to look at myself within my surroundings. If I have done something right or wrong, it is my responsibility. It is not the fault of anyone around me if I make a mistake, just as it's not to their credit if I enjoy some success. Too many times in today's world we do not take control of ourselves within our surroundings. I believe my story can project an image of self-responsibility because I have taken responsibility for who I am today.

Anyone who feels they need inspiration, whether it be an individual with a mental or physical disability, parents of children with disabilities, or someone looking to overcome an obstacle in life, can gain motivation from reading this book. It is a difficult time for many people. With the expansion of autism in our society, veterans coming back from two wars without limbs and suffering from posttraumatic stress disorder, and a growing economic crisis, there are many people out there who need a positive influence in their lives.

There is also a lesson here for the business world. I have spent most of my adult life in sales. I am proud of being a successful salesperson, while not having what one would consider an able body. There are many people out there looking for a successful sales story to motivate themselves to continue to pick up the phone, knock on doors, and achieve their sales goals. I even find myself looking for similar stories from time to time.

When I was a freshman in college, I had a difficult time making friends because I was too busy trying to impress people rather than being myself. Once I realized that I wasn't all that different from everyone else and that we all had our own personal struggles and limitations, I became the person I am—instead of who I am not—and forged some of the greatest friendships in my life.

GET OFF YOUR KNEES

1

Going for a Test Drive

> More than that, we rejoice in our sufferings,
> knowing that suffering produces endurance, and
> endurance produces character, and character
> produces hope, and hope does not disappoint
> us, because God's love has been poured into our
> hearts through the Holy Spirit which has been
> given to us.
>
> —Romans 5:3–5

SERENITY is not possible for expecting parents. We may look calm on the outside to the uninitiated, but we are terrified of the unknown. There are hundreds of questions: How will I be able to support a new life? Will my child become a good person? Will we be able to protect our child from harm? Will he or she go on to college, and how do we afford such an expense? Will my child love me? Will there be ten fingers and ten toes?

These questions—in particular, the last one—began racing through my head late one evening in early March 1997 when my wife, Andrea, revealed that she was pregnant. She had bought a small baby hat and placed it on the stuffed Velveteen Rabbit that resided on our bed. When I saw it, I looked at her, and she at me, and we both

1

smiled. Andrea had already suffered two miscarriages in the three years we had been married, but this pregnancy had a different feeling to it. She was defiant. There was going to be a birth!

There were also going to be some anxious moments ahead, and the first came shortly thereafter. At the end of the first trimester, Andrea would have her first abdominal ultrasound to see that the baby was growing and developing normally. We had not really discussed what we would do if there was a problem. Andrea had worked with people with disabilities in Ontario, and she would never terminate a pregnancy. But I was not sure I could handle a child with a physical disability, not after seeing what my parents had to go through with me. I didn't want my parents reliving their nightmare all over again, nor did I want them feeling responsible if something were indeed wrong with our child. It would have destroyed them.

Andrea and I walked into the doctor's office. The nurse recognized our apprehension and smiled. Andrea climbed onto the examining table while I backed into the corner of the small room. I was praying for a healthy picture. I was praying harder in this one moment than I had for anything else in my life. I believed this one picture had the power to heal some deep family wounds. It would provide some tangible proof of Andrea's blind faith that I could father a healthy child. It could ease the pain of not knowing if I would ever be a father.

As Andrea disrobed her small belly, I wondered, can one picture help my parents forgive themselves for my birth? I was praying for this release as well.

The monitor came to life as the nurse rubbed jelly onto the instrument and placed it on Andrea's belly. This one moment was going to tell us if we were going to follow the path of many parents during their first childbirth experience or if we were to relive what my parents went through nearly thirty years before.

My mother did not have the same opportunity for an ultrasound in 1968. What would she have done? Would she have delivered me had she known the trauma ahead? She had faith that she was going to bring a healthy child into this world. When Mom asked the anxious questions that run through the mind of every expecting parent, my father said God would provide a healthy child. He believed, as all Christians do, that if you live your life right and are faithful to God, he will protect you and allow you to prosper.

I was born on the first Sunday after Thanksgiving, December 1, 1968, which also happened to be the first Sunday in the Christian season of Advent. Mom had decided to make a large Thanksgiving meal for my father, even though they had just celebrated the holiday with relatives a few days earlier. She wanted to prepare the turkey and all the fixings herself. Mom cooked all morning to make the dinner that would be our Thanksgiving menu for years to come: turkey flushed out with bourbon, mashed potatoes, gravy, stuffing, squash, stuffed oysters, and English trifle for dessert. For twenty-six-year-old Priscilla Ann Morris Robinson, this was how life was supposed to be.

David Robinson was a twenty-seven-year-old deacon at the Trinity Memorial Church in Binghamton, having just completed a three-year baptismal ministry program at the Episcopal Divinity School in Cambridge, Massachusetts. My father claims my mom pursued him from the very beginning. They had met several years earlier at the high school in LaFayette, New York, some sixty-five miles north of Binghamton. Dad taught English literature, and Mom was a secretary to the principal. Dad was a worldly man compared to the men in LaFayette. He was college educated and about to become a minister to God's people. Mom could see herself with him. The perfect image of life shifted from farmer's wife to vicar's wife.

Dad had his own story. My grandfather was a self-taught Wesleyan Methodist minister from Canada who had spent his life preaching fire and brimstone. Whereas today's children may rebel with tattoos or ill-fitting clothing, my father's retaliation was leaving the church of his upbringing for the Anglican Church with its rich history, music, and ritual. My father felt his calling to praise God in a new way, not by spreading guilt ministry or threatening eternal damnation. His move away from the fundamentalist beliefs and rigidity of the Methodist Church ruptured their relationship. Leaving to join the Episcopal Church was akin to becoming a communist, or so my grandfather thought. The decision weighed heavily on my father, who was extremely close to my grandfather. But my dad felt an irresistible call to a new expression of his religion.

When my father fell for Mom, it was pretty much all over. I learned later through my own experience that when a woman truly loves a man, there is no stopping

1. As a curate, David Robinson prepares for the ministry at Trinity Episcopal Church in Binghamton.

that relationship. Mom became a great friend and a wonderful young wife for Dad.

Although I am sure they knew they would be together, Dad did not ask Mom to marry him. The bishop who sent Dad to theological school and counseled him on the priesthood brought up the subject. Bishop Walter Higley called Mom and Dad into his office. He pointed out how well they got along together. He asked Dad in front of Mom if he was going to ask her to marry him, and Dad said yes. That was how they were engaged.

They were married in a small ceremony the summer between Dad's first and second years of seminary. It was Mom's second marriage, but in contrast to her first, which all of LaFayette had attended, this time the family gathered on its own in a small church on the south side of Syracuse. In lieu of the larger, more traditional reception with dinner, plenty of photo ops, and dancing, my parents' reception was limited to the church. I have seen only one photo of their wedding day.

The best thing to ever happen to Mom was moving away from the farm in LaFayette, my father would later say. She experienced college vicariously through my father's seminary adjacent to the Harvard campus. The flower-child times of hippies, free love, music, and war protest were a major change for the farm girl from upstate New York. Though Mom always insisted she was conservative, she evolved into a more understanding person after her experiences in Cambridge.

Upon my father's graduation from seminary, my parents moved to Binghamton, where my father was hired as deacon—a priest in training, or apprentice—to the Reverend Paul Thompson of Trinity Episcopal Church. Binghamton was not Boston; it was a return to upstate New York, a style of life with which my mom was familiar. She was now only an hour's drive from her own mother.

My parents learned in the spring of 1968 that she was pregnant. That year of historical national turmoil—the assassinations of Martin Luther King Jr. and presidential hopeful Robert F. Kennedy, as well as the Vietnam War—paralleled the tempest growing inside.

This was my mom's first pregnancy, and she was not fully aware of the changes inside her body. She felt movements inside, as all women feel, but she had no frame of reference to realize that the movement was without limbs and I was rolling head to foot, almost like a bowling ball. As time went on, my mother's intuition triggered the question of what they would do if there was a problem. My father thought about it and answered that God would not let anything bad happen to their first child.

They had no idea what was ahead.

When Dad arrived home from church on December 1, 1968, my mother made him sit down to enjoy his post-Thanksgiving meal. She decided she didn't feel well enough to eat and went into the bedroom to rest. She was in labor. My father joined my mom for a nap but was awakened shortly thereafter because the contractions were getting very close together. They arrived at the hospital shortly after five o'clock. My mother's ob-gyn—a good family friend—was away on a hunting trip, and I was delivered by cesarean section at 9:09 P.M. by an unfamiliar doctor.

The initial silence in the room indicated immediately to my mom that something was terribly wrong. I wasn't held right away. When my mother asked about me, she was given something to sedate her. I was screaming as any newborn does those first cold moments.

Unlike today, new fathers were not allowed in the delivery room. My dad was pulled from the waiting room and told there was a problem. "You have a son," said the doctor, "but . . ." Not exactly the words you want to hear from the ob-gyn.

Dad's promise to my mother was ringing in his ears. "God will not let anything bad happen to our first child." Just that morning, he preached to the congregation about how having a child is a symbol of Christmas and the season of Advent, which means the coming or arrival of Jesus. And now he was being told there was something very wrong with his first child.

I was born a congenital amputee, without the extension of my arms and minus hands. My arms stop at the elbow. My lower legs are attached to my hips without knees. My feet are different: I have two toes on each. I am short—only three feet and nine inches at my current height. My father looked at me on that December day and thought, "How will he be able to hold things, grab a pencil, feed or dress himself? How will he walk without the balance provided by knees? Will he be able to get around? How will we deal with his needs? Why us?"

When the nurses pulled back the blankets so my father could see my arms and legs, I started to scream very loudly. My father said, "You go right ahead and scream. If anyone has the right to scream, you do."

I was a strong, vigorous baby and, with the exception of my physical disabilities, tested very healthy. But that was of little comfort to my parents at the time. They had a mental image of what their son or daughter might be, and I was not it. They had certain dreams for their child as well. In my father's case, he had a passion and a gift for music. He could play the organ, the piano, and the trombone, and he could sing. But he was not very gifted athletically, and he hoped that his child could run and play sports better than he could. Now, he was simply wondering if his child would ever walk. Those hopes and dreams—at least for the moment—were shattered.

In the days and weeks after my birth, my dad became enraged with a God who would allow such a birth. He felt guilty—was it because he had left his father's path? He questioned whether he should preach the gospel when he wasn't sure he still believed in a benevolent God. But the Reverend Thompson was a very kind, generous man of faith who gave my father the time to work through his religious crisis. Had my father still been teaching when I was born, he would have been able to work even though he questioned his beliefs. But because the church was his career, he had to deal with his conflicted feelings expeditiously and directly. He was the support that my mother needed to get through her own feelings.

My mom would not accept me the first few days in the hospital. She was in shock. She refused to hold me, nurse me, or even look at me. Nor would she see anyone: for several days there was a "No Visitors" sign on her hospital door. How would they raise me? My mother and I were very much alike. We were both strong willed.

We always held a strong connection, but at first I was not what she had envisioned.

While Dad was questioning God, my mother was questioning herself. Was this some kind of punishment? She felt guilty about having had such a child and thought perhaps my birth was proof that life was never as perfect as it seemed to be, or how she had envisioned it to be. Why were her dreams being dealt such an enormous defeat? My mother was a very emotional person. She was quick to laugh, yell, and love. Unlike my father, she left her emotions out there for everyone to see. My mother's initial reluctance to me was the first stage in dealing with her disappointment. She needed to vent and then move on.

Shortly before my parents were to take me home my father pulled the ob-gyn aside and said my mother was not coping with the situation very well. She hadn't even seen me. The doctor took me into her room, undressed me so my mom could see how I looked, and then told her to hold me. She cried and said that she didn't know what to do. The doctor then said, "You know how when you buy a new car, you don't know how it's going to perform, or how it's going to work out? What if you took him home for a while to see if he is a good fit? Take him home for a test drive. If you like him, keep him. If not, bring him back."

As if they could bring me back! The doctor's words were the push that my mom needed to bring her new baby home.

My parents did a great job in raising me. When we later moved to New Hampshire, family friends had a child born with a mental disability. They named their son

2. With my mother, Priscilla, around 1976. The portrait was taken by a family friend. The appendage on the end of my left arm is affectionately referred to as the "marshmallow."

John. They told my parents that if their child could only turn out as well as I did, then they would be lucky. As an adult, I have had friends tell me they will keep whatever child God provides them. I was their inspiration that any life is worth protecting.

The ob-gyn advised my parents to be the best parents they could be. The way to do so was to ignore the disability as often as they could, to challenge and nurture me the same way a parent would any child.

My parents lived this test-driven mentality every day and instilled it in me. I have challenged myself subconsciously to look past my disability and become the best person I can be, not to use my disability as a crutch. I have always wanted to be seen as others are seen in the eyes of my superiors and peers. Able-bodied people are my measuring stick.

When my sister, Katherine, was born two and a half years later, she became my motivation. My parents were not sure I was ever going to be able to walk without assistance, but when my sister started to crawl, I craved the attention she was now getting. So I started to walk on my own. It wasn't until I had someone to push me that I developed the urgency to walk.

3. This walker's legs were bent out to lower the height so my legs could reach the floor. It was vital in teaching me how to walk and run.

My mother and father decided early on to fit me with artificial arms and legs. They met with a specialist in New Jersey from the time I was two weeks old until I turned twelve. Just as every parent has to buy their child new shoes as his or her feet grow, mine had to get new arms and legs made for me. My dad says I would scream each time the plaster casts were removed because I was afraid of the saw used to cut through the

4. Wearing my artificial arms in front of my toy piano and tractor at our home in Binghamton.

plaster and he would have to hold me down. I hated those trips!

I believe my father's anguish during these doctor visits caused some stress on my parents' marriage over the years. Eventually, my father would make these trips alone or with a friend, and my mom would stay at home. My father shouldered most of the direct stress from schools, activities, and doctors, and it took a toll on him. My mother was loud and emotional, whereas my dad was more introspective and quiet. He kept his feelings and pain hidden, pouring them into his vocation in the priesthood. It is a true testament to my parents' test-driven mentality that they were able to work through their disagreements about me. They worked through their own problems, all the while showing me how to work through mine.

The *test* in *test drive* really defines who I am. I cannot travel through life along the same path, content with who I am; I'm constantly challenging myself to be better—as a parent, a person, a salesman, a golfer, and so on. Back in the doctor's office on that day in 1997, my biggest personal test was about to arrive. Standing there as the nurse administered the sonogram to Andrea, I was wondering if we would face the same challenges my parents did. I prayed that we would be told there was no problem, although I rationalized that because of all I went through as a child I would have a better perspective in raising a child with a disability.

When the monitor came to life, I did not know what I was looking at. I was searching for fingers and toes, while the nurse was looking for a heartbeat. She was searching around, taking measurements, when I finally asked, "How does the baby look?" She said everything was fine and pointed out feet and hands. What a wonderful feeling! I started to cry. I was struck by how unfair that moment on December 1, 1968, had been for my parents. For the first time in my life, I allowed myself to think about the emotions they had experienced.

When Andrea and I got home, like most expectant parents, we called our parents. I explained to them that our future child looked healthy. The baby had fingers and toes, hands and feet, and looked to be of normal size. I was proud to announce it yet a little sad. The news must

5. With my daughter, Ariel, shortly after her birth in November 1997.

have reminded them of how unprepared they were the night I was born.

After Ariel was born on November 5, 1997, I could hear thirty years of pain diminish when I let my parents know she was okay. My mom cried tears of joy and relief on the telephone. My dad called me later that night, I'm sure after reliving my birth in his mind. He asked me if I was okay; all the while I was wondering the same about him. He asked me if I felt cheated at all because of the way I entered the world. I said I no longer did. I realized for the first time it was truly an act of God. I said that I appreciated this birth that much more because of my perspective. I was blessed with a healthy child and appreciated how well my parents dealt with my birth.

2

REFLECTION

AS A YOUNG PRIEST, my father spent almost as much time entertaining guests at home as he did preaching in church. Most of these visitors were other priests or friends of the church, and it was not uncommon for them to spend the night at our home.

One of these friends was David Whitmore. David arrived in Greene, New York, in June 1975 on his way to Nova Scotia. A free spirit and worldly traveler, David was a lifelong friend of Sally Gould, the church organist at Zion Episcopal Church where my dad preached. Sally and David were from Modesto, California, a small city ninety miles east of San Francisco, and had met as kids in church. But David was not your typical beach boy from California. He was born with major deformities in his knees and lower legs. His adoptive mother, who worked in a facility for children with disabilities, raised David and three adopted siblings. Eventually, she decided that both of David's deformed legs would have to be amputated at the knees so that he would be able to walk around on his stumps.

Sally had explained my physical disability to David. She has always been a very intuitive individual, and she knew that if she told David about my condition, he would take a keen interest in me. It didn't matter that I was only six years old.

It was explained to me that David wore his prosthetic legs when he desired to be the same height as other people, and the rest of the time he wore a simple rubber "boot" on the end of each leg, similar to the stopper on the bottom of a cane. Sally said he liked to run around in the rubber boots because the artificial legs caused him too much pain. So when he traveled the globe from San Francisco to Nova Scotia to India, he usually did so in his rubber boots. His physical limitations did not stop him from seeking out adventure.

I remember David's visit to this very day. It was my first recollection of meeting somebody with a physical disability like myself. As David later said, it was something I needed. When he walked into the house, he had his prosthetic legs on under his pants. At first glance, David Whitmore looked no different to me than any other adult.

Later, I was called up to the guest room where David was staying. As I entered the room, he stood on the ends of his amputated legs. He asked if I wanted to race, and before I knew it we took off down the hallway with our short-legged gaits. It wasn't your typical footrace, but it sure was fun!

Until that moment, I had never met an amputee outside of the New Jersey hospital that fitted me for my artificial arms and legs, nor had I given much thought to fellow amputees. But I do remember the curiosity I had when David and I met for the first time. It gave me a sense of comfort and confidence to see another amputee moving around so well without the aid of prosthetics. When I think about it, I'm sure that's a big reason my parents encouraged him to visit—to be a physical example of someone who "made it" with prosthetics.

Allow me to backtrack now and explain in definitive terms what I am physically. Until recently, I was under the impression that I was born a congenital amputee. Today, the term is slightly different—*congenital limb loss,* or *difference*—although in my mind it's the same. Congenital limb loss refers to the absence of a fetal limb or fetal part at birth, such as hands or feet. It is very rare to have a complete limb loss. Doctors acknowledge that children are most likely to have their arms affected by these birth defects, not their legs. Rarely is it bilateral (that is, affecting both the arms and the legs). However, in my case, it was: I was born with half arms and shortened legs. My arms resemble what you might see with a war veteran who has had his arms amputated; my legs have little comparison to anything.

According to amputee-coalition.org as well as marchofdimes.com, there are approximately 1.7 million people with limb loss in the United States—excluding fingers and toes. But there are relatively few people born with congenital limb loss. In 1996 it was recorded as 25.64 per 100,000 live births. I always knew intuitively it was a small number, but imagine my surprise at just how small of a number. And the number of babies who suffer congenital limb loss to all four limbs is even smaller. I seem to have hit the jackpot!

It was explained to me that the development of my bone structure at five weeks of gestation was hindered. It's at this point in the first trimester of pregnancy that the extremities of the bones are finally formed; it also happens to be when some of the teeth are formed, and I am missing my two upper eye teeth. They mysteriously did not arrive when all of my other teeth came in, which, according to one of the doctors, occurred at about five weeks. I am blessed that I am not missing more than just those two teeth.

The development of my arms stopped at the elbows. I have no elbows, forearms, wrists, or hands to speak of; however, the nerve endings that form at the start of the hands and fingers are still present. At least, I think they are. Although I can't wiggle any fingers or make a fist, it feels as if I can. I know how my hands would operate because I can not only feel the muscles at the end of each arm but make them move.

On the base of my left arm, where most people would have their thumb pad, is a round lump of muscle tissue that my friends affectionately refer to as the "marshmallow." My college roommate Pat Kelleher always thought that this marshmallow was surgically attached to my arm so that I would be able to open doors. Although it's not true, it's a great observation. Without this small appendage, I would not be able to carry out a variety of functions, like balancing a fork or cell phone, opening and closing a door, shuffling through pages of a book or newspaper, or grabbing a steering wheel. I have heard other people over the years wonder how this marshmallow got there. I'm not quite sure how it did; I'm just very grateful it's there. It works about as well as a normal thumb.

My legs are remarkably different. The femoral head, the upper part of the thigh bone also known as the ball of the hip, is not fully developed. So there is no ball riding up into my hip socket. If you were to make a fist with your right hand and put it into your cupped left hand, that's what the X-ray of a normal hip bone and socket joint would look like. The femoral head would be your fist. However, there is no such fist in my hip. It's been replaced by what my general practitioner speculates is fatty tissue, or the beginning of cartilage. He is perplexed as to what it is but recommends that I see specialists just to create a reference point. Whatever it is, it's all that's holding my hip together.

My hips are larger than most people's because my femoral bone rides high and also juts out to the side. Over the past five to ten years I have experienced more hip pain than I ever have before, and my doctor is worried about how we might correct it if we ever need to. Because I have no knees, normal hip replacement would require me to learn how to walk again. The reason I walk side to side is because I don't have the knee-bending movement required to pull my leg up for the next step. I have to shuffle my legs from side to side to move them.

I do not have ankle joints. It's as if my lower legs were attached to my hips. I have no thighs. I am, however, blessed with two feet. David Whitmore did not have this luxury—both of his legs were deformed below his knees without feet. If he had two feet, then perhaps his mother would've decided against surgery, but as it turns out, surgery was necessary so that he could walk. I am thankful every day that my feet face forward (I have seen other congenital amputees with feet that face backward) and that I am able to walk on them. In addition, I have two toes on each foot—a big toe and one of the second toes. The big toe on my right foot is significantly bent but is still very helpful in gripping the ground and providing balance.

My feet are a boy's or young man's size 4, which makes it difficult to find shoes. Thankfully, Doc Martens out of England still produces shoes in this size. However, finding a pair of golf shoes that are not children's width is about as easy as making birdie. My feet are normal width, but sometimes children's shoes are narrower. I seem to run or walk best in cross-trainer or basketball shoes that are not high tops. Because of my shuffling motion, my feet do scuffle on the floor at times, and if I have a high tread, my heels will strike the ground first.

In reading how congenital limb loss usually affects the arms or legs, but rarely both, I find it ironic that I've been dealt with a four-limbed amputation. Maybe life would be a lot different with two full limbs. Maybe not. I've thought of every scenario, but as strange as it might seem, I feel quite lucky that my limb loss is proportional. So while I may stand only three feet nine inches tall, I'm a proportional three-foot-nine.

There are all sorts of reasons that natural amputation occurs, from genetics and environmental pollutants to illness and pharmaceutical drugs. I've heard them all in discussions about what caused my congenital limb loss. Both of my parents underwent genetic counseling prior to my sister Katherine's birth in 1971, and doctors all but ruled out genetics as a cause at that time. The explanation I was given as a child was that my mother was exposed to rubella (commonly known as German measles) during pregnancy, although in my adult years many doctors dismissed that as a cause.

The drug Thalidomide, which doctors openly prescribed to expectant mothers to relieve symptoms of morning sickness, caused a startling number of birth defects in the late 1950s and early '60s before it was withdrawn in 1961. According to the March of Dimes, there were more than ten thousand births with major deformities in the early 1960s due to Thalidomide. Of course, since I was born in 1968, that drug had nothing to do with my condition. My mother did not take it. In fact, following my birth, the pharmaceutical company responsible for Thalidomide wanted my parents to speak out on its behalf to say that physical disabilities can happen to anyone. My parents refused.

It's never really mattered to me why. I subscribe to the theory that "it's just a fluke of nature," as one doctor put it. That very same doctor asked me as an adult if I was going to worry about it to the point that I didn't want to have children. "Wouldn't you try anyway?" he asked. "Couldn't you raise a child with an amputation if that's what was in God's plan?" "Of course," I said, and it's possible I would be better equipped to handle such a situation than other parents would. Then again, maybe the pain would be twice as intense for me as it would be for other parents, because of the responsibility I would feel for such a birth.

I didn't ask why, but my mother and father had their struggles with my disability, as did my sister, Katherine, later on. This situation is not unusual at all, for the burden is often felt most by the people around us. In a 2006 article in *inMotion,* a leading amputee publication, Douglas G. Smith, M.D., describes congenital limb loss: "Limb loss is especially devastating whenever it happens to a child. Sometimes, limb loss in children results from birth defects, cancer or severe infections. In other cases, a traumatic injury from a lawn mower or traffic accident is the reason. Limb loss deeply affects the child and his or her brothers and sisters."

Dr. Smith hints of the family's burden in his quote. My parents had many questions early on. Why them? Why me? Shortly after my birth, my mother wasn't sure if she would ever be able to hold me. My father openly questioned his faith at a time when he was just getting started as a priest. As my sister got older, she had a hard time dealing with my disability and its place in our family. She was not only my sister but also my part-time caregiver. She was there to help dress me when I was unable to, reach items that I could not reach, and assist me when I was unable to carry something. There were many instances when her physical being helped me in my daily life. But she also felt the burden of having to help when asked. She was jealous of the attention I

6. My sister, Katherine, and I play in the raked leaves at our house in Greene in 1976. Katherine was born in March 1971.

received from my parents, and she became increasingly frustrated with my disability.

The irony is that of the four of us, I was the one least likely to ask, "Why?" I didn't really think about my disability all that much because I was living with it, and trying to lead my life. My parents and sister quietly struggled with the fact that they were able-bodied and I wasn't. They wondered how it could happen to me and not them. But when you think about it, it's very normal. Oftentimes when a family member is sick or gravely ill, it's the children or spouse who feel a tremendous burden. It was true when my mother contracted Lou Gehrig's disease. I watched in horror as this debilitating disease weakened my mother to the point that she couldn't walk or feed herself. In this instance, the burden was on me, my sister, and my dad. We had to take care of her, but we also had to deal with the reality that she'd be leaving us and we'd have to go on without her. And there was that question of why. Why did it have to happen to her?

The burden is lifted when you're among other amputees, however. It's rare I meet someone with a similar condition, so when I do, I can't help but ask a lot of questions. I like to share stories with other amputees to find out how they've done things. There's a feeling of camaraderie with them that I don't experience with everyone else, because they know what it's like to go through life without an arm or a leg. And there's no emotional baggage attached. Just as it's easy for one cancer survivor to talk to another, it's easy for me to sit down with another amputee and discuss our histories, as well as our successes and failures.

As with David Whitmore, I've been very impressed by the other amputees I've met and how they've been able to adapt similarly. I play cards with a man in Albany who is missing a hand. He holds his playing cards in his good hand and adjusts them with the end of his deformed hand, similar to what I do. And although I never met him, I watched with great admiration as Jim Abbott succeeded in pitching in the major leagues despite being born without his right hand. Abbott not only won eighty-seven big-league games over his career but threw a no-hitter against the Cleveland Indians while pitching for my beloved New York Yankees in 1993. Abbott was one of my role models later in life, just as David Whitmore was in my early years.

Another person with a disability who inspired me was former U.S. senator Bob Dole. I had the opportunity to see Mr. Dole speak at our high school in New Hampshire in the late 1980s, when he was running for the Republican presidential nomination. I was struck by his physical appearance and how little his right arm and hand moved (later I learned that his right arm was badly injured by German machine-gun fire in World War II, which left the arm partially paralyzed). I was equally struck by how he never mentioned it. Even in 1996, when he ran for president against Democratic nominee Bill Clinton, he didn't discuss his disability unless asked about it.

I'm dumbfounded that there are so few role models for people with disabilities—specifically amputees—especially with so many soldiers coming back from Iraq as amputees. With Dole, here was somebody who could've been a role model for all people with disabilities and should have been a role model. Although I can understand his discomfort, I do believe he had an opportunity to discuss something of a personal nature that would have connected with many people.

Later in my adult years I had the opportunity to meet actor Meinhardt Raabe, who played the coroner in the 1939 classic *The Wizard of Oz*. One of the oldest surviving Munchkins, Raabe was being interviewed at the television station where I worked in Syracuse, WSTM. The village of Chittenango, which is a short drive from Syracuse, hosts a *Wizard of Oz* convention each summer to celebrate

L. Frank Baum's writing of the fabled book (Baum was born in Chittenango). Raabe was the actor who gloriously announced, "The witch is dead!"

As Raabe was being interviewed, I had a long chat with his wife, Margaret. They were the first two adults I had ever met who were my height. I always noticed other people and their disabilities but had never met anybody who stood three feet nine inches tall. How great it was to be able to look eye to eye with somebody!

3

Running on Faith

God grant me the serenity to accept the things I cannot
change, courage to change the things I can, and wisdom to
know the difference.
—"Serenity Prayer," Rienhold Niebuhr

FAITH RUNS DEEP throughout my life. Faith in God, faith
in myself, and faith in mankind have all come together to
make me the person I am today.

Chief among them has been my faith in God, which
I inherited from my father and a family of preachers
extending back to the mid-nineteenth century. It was
my maternal great-grandfather, Adam Joseph Shea of
Prescott, Ontario, a Wesleyan Church minister, who per-
suaded my grandfather Harvey Robinson to leave the
family's farm in Waltham, Quebec, and make preaching
his calling in life. He later married Mary Shea, one of
eight children from Ottawa, Ontario, the most famous of
whom is George Beverly Shea. For more than sixty years,
Uncle Bev served as the personal gospel soloist for the
Reverend Billy Graham—the famous Evangelical Christian minister and TV personality—and his crusades.
Uncle Bev, who turned one hundred in February 2009,

recorded more than seventy albums of religious music, and was inducted into the Gospel Music Hall of Fame in 1978. Grandma Mary Shea died two years ago, but not before she lived to see one hundred as well.

Faith in God was the only way of life for both of my grandmothers. My maternal grandmother, Helen Morris, spent most of her adult life as a farmer's wife and mother. Because women in the early to mid-1900s weren't encouraged or allowed to pursue a career outside of the home, her only form of expression was to write in her journal about her belief in Jesus and the gospel. She was self-educated in theology, and she had little trouble holding her own in conversations with my father, an Episcopal priest, and my uncle Karl Esmark, a Presbyterian minister.

She was a big follower of Billy Graham, which was a bit ironic since my mother and father were not fundamentalist in any way. My father split from the Wesleyan Methodist Church shortly after graduating from Houghton College, a Christian school of liberal arts and sciences in western New York, in 1963. He began to feel his own call to the ministry, but it wasn't in his father's tradition. Dad was uncomfortable with the strict ways of the Wesleyan Methodist Church, which had stern rules about drinking, smoking, and dating and was largely resistant to change. The Wesleyan Methodists believe you have to be born again as an adult, so anytime someone entered my grandfather's home, they had to express out loud their belief in Jesus Christ. It was too rigid for my father. He searched for a new expression of faith and found it with the Episcopal Church.

A descendant of the Church of England, the Episcopal Church differs from the Wesleyan Methodist Church
in that it follows the body of teachings of the twelve
apostles, or disciples, of Jesus, who founded the Christian
Church. It preaches the gospel of the church, or what my
father refers to as the three-legged stool—biblical teachings, the history of the church, and reason—whereas the
Wesleyan Methodist Church follows its own interpretation of the Bible. The local priest preaches straight out of
the Bible based on his own interpretation of the Bible, not
through the historical doctrines of the Bible.

My father's decision to leave the Methodist Church
created a great rift between him and my granddad. They
barely spoke to one another, and as I grew up I had little
contact with my paternal grandparents or anyone else on
my dad's side of the family. My dad, however, occasionally
watched Billy Graham to hear Uncle Bev sing, and that's
when I started to realize that I had a very famous uncle. I
got to meet Uncle Bev only one time, as a teenager at a family reunion of the Sheas at Houghton College in the mid-
1980s. I'm sure he had heard much about my life from my
grandmother, whom I spoke with on the phone on occasion, and he embraced me with the love of a lifelong friend.
He congratulated me on how far I'd come and was over-
joyed that Jesus Christ was such a big part of my life. Here
was this world-renowned gospel singer telling me how
much he cared and that things would turn out okay for me
because my faith was strong. It was awfully nice to hear.

I was baptized at Trinity Church in Binghamton,
New York, when I was two weeks old, even though my

father, still studying to become a priest, was having a crisis of faith. He had told my mother that God would not let anything happen to their child, and out I came—a biblical slap in the face to his faith. My father was confused and resentful. "Where is God in this," he asked his rector, the Reverend Paul Thompson, "and how could there be a God that would allow this sort of thing to happen?" He wasn't sure he could preach the gospel anymore.

The Reverend Thompson was a man of tremendous faith and a great mentor to my father. In response to my dad's questions about where God was, he said, "Well, I don't know what God is doing, but I know what God's people are doing, and that is praying and sending flowers and food and treating you as if you were one of their own families." This statement is the very essence of why you go to an Episcopal church. You are part of a community; you are brothers and sisters in life, and you are together in good times and bad. The church—the whole church—is the body of Christ in the world, and it suffers with him and tries to heal with him.

The people of Trinity Episcopal Church were amazing during those first few weeks and months of my life. They would come by with meals, help with the laundry, even stay with me so my mother could get some much needed rest. My mom was never alone. As my father said to me later, "They cared for us and took us in." I began my life in a Christian community of several hundred people who were very loving and caring toward me and my parents. This fact, more than anything, helped ease my father's burden and restore his faith.

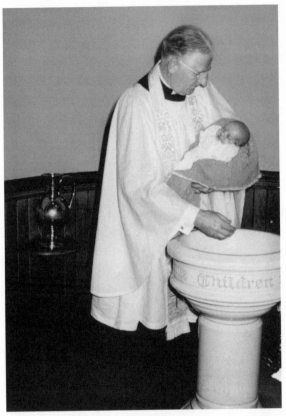

7. I was baptized by the Reverend Paul Thompson on December 15, 1968, at Trinity Episcopal Church in Binghamton, New York. I was two weeks old.

It was as if I had two families growing up—one included my parents and later my sister, Katherine, and the other was the church community. There was always someone who sat with me as I listened to my dad's sermons. I paid more attention to what was being said in church than I did in school, which wasn't lost on the people of the church—the organist, choir, ushers, and others. They had my respect, and I had theirs, to the point that they would often look to me if they had any questions about what was next in the service. I was so well versed in the theology and etiquette of the church that at age nine I took the unusual step of seeking confirmation.

It was my insistence to advance the traditional age for confirmation, which was thirteen at the time. There were many who wanted to push this age back, since so many kids would be confirmed and then stop coming to church or Sunday school, especially after college, but I felt the need to become a bigger part of the church. I asked to join the confirmation class my father was teaching, and went through the whole series of lessons and prayers. I, as the Episcopal rubric required, knew the Lord's Prayer and the Ten Commandments, and indicated that I would follow Jesus as my Lord and Savior. The sitting bishop of the diocese presides over the confirmation, and on the eve of the ceremony, Bishop Ned Cole arrived in Greene and spent the night at our house. It was unusual because most other clergymen stayed in motels.

My father says I was a very good reader and smart and had no trouble with the preparations. But Bishop Cole thought I was too young to seek full membership into the church. When my father told me, I was devastated and started to cry. I didn't understand the bishop's verdict, because I had gone through all of the classes, just like everyone else, and it meant so much to me. My father said to me, "If you really want to be confirmed tomorrow,

go into the living room and ask him yourself personally."
I went in and made my case directly to the bishop. I don't
remember what I said, but it must have been persuasive.
The bishop changed his mind, and I was confirmed the
next day.

We remained part of the central New York church
community until 1980, when my father took the head
priest job at Grace Episcopal Church in Manchester, New
Hampshire. I spent much of my following teenage years
bonding with my father. During Lent season—a period
of forty days between Ash Wednesday and Easter Sunday—the Episcopal Church would rotate Wednesday-
evening services, and my dad would serve as a guest
priest at various Episcopal churches throughout New
Hampshire. One of my greatest joys was to be with my
father during this time, traveling with him to and from
each service, listening to him preach and meeting new
people. It was time I got to spend alone with him, which
was rare. My father wasn't a big sports fan, like I was, and
he didn't take much of an interest in my schoolwork, so
the only way to really spend quality time with him was
at his job. As we traveled to these different parishes, I got
to see firsthand how much he enjoyed his work and cared
about people. I idolized my father.

Ironically, I wound up learning more about my personal faith during this period than at any other point
in my life. Junior high and high school were difficult
times for me. I was trying to be a normal teenager
while still learning to cope with my physical disability. I was overweight and self-conscious, and I had no

girlfriends. I didn't play any sports or participate in many school-related activities, so there was no real outlet for me except in my own mind.

I drew a personal strength from the church that I didn't get from school. I listened intently to what was said—through my dad, the readings, the music and prayer—and the message was clear: if you believed, you worked hard, and you were a good person, the path would be shown to you. I realized that there was a path for me and it could be anything I wanted it to be, but first I had to develop the self-faith and self-confidence to meet the challenges that lay ahead of me.

Prayer was a big part of my daily life and meeting those challenges. When we lived in Greene, a needlepoint hung on my bedroom wall (and later the dining room) embroidered with the "Serenity Prayer." As a young child I never paid much attention to the words in the prayer, but as I traveled with my dad to these weekly services, I started to think more about their meaning: "The serenity to accept the things I cannot change." I cannot change how I look, or how I appear in other people's eyes. "The courage to change the things I can." I can change how I react to people and the perceptions they have of me, and with the help of a good education I can pursue my own path and dreams. "The wisdom to know the difference." This is the hardest part. The words change every day because some of the things you can't alter now you can affect later. I believe I am here with this body for a purpose. I am not sure what the purpose is even to this day; it's the journey that will define who I am to be.

8. A portrait of the Reverend David Robinson taken in the mid-1970s while serving as rector at Zion Episcopal Church in Greene, New York.

When my daughter, Ariel, was born, I asked my parents if they could get me a copy of the "Serenity Prayer" that hung in our living room. I wanted her to gain strength and hope from that prayer, just as I did. Today, it hangs in the front hallway of our home outside Albany, just beside her baby picture.

I'm sure my parents' faith in God was questioned in the days and months following my birth. I'm sure both sets of grandparents wondered why God could create such a situation for a young child. I'm sure they didn't mention that among themselves but privately questioned, "Why?" At the same time, it was their faith in God that helped them get through that time. It was my parents' faith in God that guided them to raise me the way they did and got me to think about what I believe in.

I've had many friends ask me if I believe in God. It's not something that I openly preach about, but when asked I don't hesitate to tell them, "Yes, I do." It does me no good to be mad at God or mad at the world because of my physical disability. There are hundreds of thousands of people born every year with mental and physical disabilities. I believe that I'm here for a purpose in life. I believe in the Anglican Church. I believe we can all have a great impact on our society if we work hard and have faith in ourselves.

I have become a spiritual leader for many of my closest friends. One has asked me about God, and what his role can be in his life. I offer as much as I can. Here is a person who has dealt with a lot of tragedy in his life. He lost his older brother to suicide in high school, survived his parents' divorce, and had a college classmate perish aboard PanAm Flight 103 over Lockerbie, Scotland, in 1988. There were thirty-five Syracuse University students aboard the doomed airplane, many from my junior class. My friend has asked me in the past about baptism. He is not baptized and would like to be. When he and his fiancée were to be married, he asked me to find a way to marry them. They even found a Web site where I could become an ordained minister.

Another of my close friends is Jewish. He, too, has suffered a tremendous amount of tragedy in his life, losing a brother to skin cancer in his thirties and his closest friend to the attack on the World Trade Center on September 11, 2001. His oldest son suffers from autism. He and I talk about faith, but it's different from religious faith. We discuss where we are in life, what we're doing, what we believe in, and what our plans are for the future. At the end of the day, we are very like-minded in that we're really grateful for what we have. When you go through difficult times as he and I have, you feel even more blessed for what you do have, not just what you miss. I have tried hard to understand Judaism through my friends' faith, even at times offending them. I have never meant any offense but realize that in learning you sometimes ask ridiculous questions. All people can be close-minded toward different faiths at times, but I do try to respect everyone's beliefs.

Faith in God and myself has given me the power to deal with my disability. It has taught me how to solve problems that arise in everyday life, and have the courage (and determination) to walk into a meeting at three feet nine inches tall and get business associates to listen to what I have to say. It has afforded me the patience and strength to be the parent of three wonderful children. My faith allows me to continue to meet every challenge I face, to adapt to a world built for able-bodied individuals. I take that knowledge forward, knowing that with a little bit of thought and hard work I should be able to adapt to any situation.

At the same time, it's my faith in other people that allows me to ask for assistance when it's needed. For the first eighteen years of my life, it was mostly family that provided me with this help, but as I moved on to college and later joined the workforce, I had to lean on this faith in others more heavily. I believe that people are inherently good and want to do good, which is why I don't overreact when a client or individual has an uneasy or adverse reaction to me when we first meet. I have confidence that I can turn around someone's initial perception and make them my friend or business associate, provided they're willing to give me a chance.

You have to believe that everyone wants what's best for themselves and their family, and that they would choose not to harm others. If you didn't, it would be an awfully dark opinion of the world. Even after PanAm 103, as awful as it was, my classmates and I all looked at each other and realized how grateful we were for our friendships and the opportunities that lay ahead of us. It didn't diminish the remaining time we had at Syracuse; if anything, it made us treasure the time we spent there even more.

Not too long ago my father told me that my birth, though excruciating at times for him and my mom, wound up being a blessing in the long run and deeply enriched their lives. He said there were strong parallels to my life and the message of suffering leading to joy that he preached about so many times in church. On the cross, Jesus said, "Why have you forsaken me? Why am I the chosen one?"

"Why me?" I have thought about that question many times, but the only true answer lies in the journey ahead. It will show itself only as time goes on. It doesn't matter if you're physically disabled, depressed, unemployed, unhappy in love, or frustrated with your job: you have to believe in yourself. You have to believe that you can accomplish what you want and that your path is the right one.

It doesn't come easy. In high school I had a strong belief in God, and in college that belief was accompanied by a faith in mankind that I could find some friends and commonality with other people. It wasn't until those two building blocks were in place that I had the self-faith and self-confidence needed to tackle the world. It was only then that I truly believed I could accomplish anything I set my mind to. It starts with believing in yourself, and for me the foundation was believing in God and the people around me.

4

LEARNING HOW
TO PRIORITIZE

MY MOM AND DAD treated me as any parent would a
normal, healthy young boy. I received no preferential
treatment; I was expected to perform my chores, do my
homework, and go to bed when they asked. At the same
time, I was encouraged to play ball with the other neighborhood kids and do what boys do, which is raise havoc
and have fun. It was never, "You can't do it because you're
disabled." They allowed me to be whatever I wanted to
be; they were not overly protective, nor did they put limitations on me because I was different. This point would
be extremely important as I became an adult, because by
not shielding me from the rest of the world, they were
preparing me for the difficult challenges that lay ahead.
I was forced to find solutions to problems—such as writing with a pencil, brushing my teeth, throwing a baseball,
walking up and down stairs—that most children don't
think twice about. If my parents did all of those things for
me, I'm not sure where I'd be today.

I adapted to the world as best I could. It was those
instances when the world had to adapt to me—such as

9. At the beach in North Bay, Ontario. I was four.

when the assistant principal or nurse at school would help me dress and undress to use the bathroom—that I felt "disabled." Nothing caused me more discomfort and humility, however, than having to wear artificial arms and legs. From the time I was six months old until I was a teenager, my father and I would make the twice-yearly drive from Greene, New York, to East Orange, New Jersey, so I could get fitted for my prosthetics. Despite my physical disability, I grew about as fast as most boys, so I needed new arms and legs about as often as I needed new shoes or jeans. This journey was no trip to the department store, however. The doctor would make a cast of my arm or leg, reproduce it, and then attach the artificial part to the end of it. The big issue for me was when the original mold, made of plaster of paris, hardened and they had to remove it. The doctor would break the cast, but not before he used a circular saw to cut through a good portion of it. It frightened me more than any needle or boogeyman ever could. I hated the process, and those trips definitely put a strain on my parents' relationship. My mom did not want to see the emotional stress. It was hard on me and would have been worse for her.

At the time, with so many disabled veterans coming back from Vietnam, it was a common occurrence to get fitted for artificial limbs. I was an amputee just as they were, except I was born with my condition. My parents didn't give it a second thought, and as much as I preferred tossing the prosthetics to the neighborhood dogs, I was

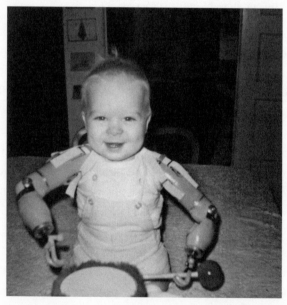

10. Here, I'm using my artificial arms to hold a drumstick at my maternal grandparents' home in LaFayette.

required to wear them to school. (The only exceptions were during gym and the writing portions of class, when I was allowed to remove the arms.) I sported these artificial limbs until the seventh grade before I was finally able to convince my parents and the prep school I attended at the time that I was better off without them. My junior high school and later my senior year high school, the Derryfield School in Manchester, New Hampshire, was unable to move everything to one floor to accommodate me—the library was upstairs and the cafeteria downstairs from the main floor, and they had no elevators. I was more mobile going up and down the stairs without my prosthetics and, thus, less likely to fall and get hurt.

I resented my fake limbs, because besides being very cumbersome and difficult to use, they stopped me from feeling like I was like the other kids. The great irony is that you put artificial arms and legs on because you want to be closer to what other kids—or adults—look like. You want to be their height. The reality was just the opposite: I stopped believing I was one of the other kids because I couldn't move as fast or run around and play ball. I didn't feel like it was me. And if I fell down, I couldn't get back up without someone's assistance. I didn't like asking for help. I had to worry about every step I took because I was walking around on stilts. Imagine if you were ten feet tall and had to walk around on five-foot stilts. It wasn't much fun. Getting up and down stairs proved to be nearly impossible because I was unable to grab the railing with my arms and pull myself up; the hook on the end of the prosthetic arm would slide up and down the railing.

11. Wearing my artificial legs for a series of family photographs taken in the living room of our home in Greene. This photo was taken around 1974.

There were only a few other instances where my physical handicap really bothered me. When I was in first grade, I was eager to join the Cub Scouts. As a member of the local pack, we were required to wear the basic uniform, which included a short-sleeve blue shirt, matching trousers or shorts, a belt and belt buckle, and a neckerchief. Naturally, my parents dressed me before each meeting because I couldn't buckle my pants or tie my neckerchief. But one day, the troop leaders made us all undress and dress as a group, and I couldn't do it. My father was infuriated because I was humiliated in such a public way; I was distraught because I didn't get the badge to put on my uniform. My Cub Scout days were over.

My failure to meet the Cub Scouts' standards wasn't totally unexpected because they made you participate in many outdoor activities that required the use of hands. Baseball was a different story. I learned to hit the ball pretty well by the time I joined T-ball because my grandfather would toss me thousands of tennis balls and baseballs in my grandparents' driveway back in LaFayette, New York. I also played a lot of Wiffle ball with my next-door neighbors in Greene. I figured out how to field and throw the ball: I'd put the glove on my left arm, catch the ball, steady it against my chin with my right arm, and then roll the ball down my arm and fling it wherever I wanted. The process of transferring the ball from my glove to my free arm wasn't all that much different from what former Major League Baseball pitcher Jim Abbott did, except Abbott, who played despite being born without a right hand, had a full arm to throw with!

Throwing a baseball was challenging for me because its size made it harder to balance and grip than a football. A lot of times, my throws would just skip along the ground. But that was okay, since I was playing second base and it was a short toss to first. In T-ball, someone pitches to you until you put the ball in play or take four balls out of the strike zone, at which point you then hit off a tee. I was adept at hitting live pitching or batting off a tee; it didn't matter. I would grip the bat between my two armpits and swing away. In my final T-ball game, I went two for three. Unfortunately, I was never allowed to play at the next level, Little League, because league officials were afraid I would get hurt. And they were unwilling to accommodate me, even though I didn't need a pinch runner and I could play the field. I was crushed!

Kids picked on me because of my physical disability, but it was never my peers, always the younger or older kids. Their actions didn't bother me all that much, because as I learned much later in life, kids' reactions to me are very unfiltered: they say what's on their minds, with no hesitation. Among my peers, I had three very close friends growing up in Greene. There were my neighbors, Chip Cooper and Kyle Eastwood—whose claim to fame was being the fourth cousin of actor Clint Eastwood— and my closest friend, Dane Clark. Chip and I probably spent the most time together, even though he was a year younger than myself. He'd ride his bike, and I'd tag along in my Big Wheel because I couldn't handle a bike. We also played Wiffle ball and basketball, and I'd even ride a skateboard, balancing myself on my tummy. Kyle was definitely the toughest of the three, probably because he lost his father at a very young age in a motorcycle accident. He was more into toys than he was sports, although all three of us enjoyed sledding down the hills behind our homes in the winter.

12. Pushing my tricycle down the street in Greene with a determined look on my face.

Dane lived out in the country, so I would frequently spend the day at his house or vice versa. He had a fort in the woods and a small fishing pond, so we'd spend most of the days outside playing. If we were inside, we liked to build things with Lincoln Logs and Legos; we never watched TV or played video games. Dane's family owned a cow, and one day while we were out fishing by the pond the animal mistook my dirty-blonde hair for hay and started grazing on my head. Dane and his family thought it was the funniest thing they had ever seen, although I'm not sure the cow was too happy with his meal.

I was generally a very happy, outgoing kid, the son of a farmer's daughter–turned–preacher's wife. As the first lady of Zion Episcopal Church in Greene, my mom had little choice but to be social, whether it was getting involved in the church choir or attending various community functions with my dad. And she enjoyed it; my mother thrived around other people, and she needed them to make her happy. She encouraged me to get out of the house and make friends, and she was the one who got me interested in sports. Where my dad worried about the big picture with me—How's he going to eat? Dress? Move around? How's he going to have any kind of life?—my mom was concerned only with getting me through each day. She wasn't worried about tomorrow. The irony is that by encouraging me to be more outgoing, she was preparing me for the future. I would not be the salesperson I am today without the social skills my mom taught me as a child.

My mom was no softy, however. When I was out of the house, I was free to do whatever I wanted to, but when I was inside I was expected to vacuum, clean my room, and pitch in around the house. That was the farmer's girl in her: you did your chores, and you made no bones about it; you did what you were told. Both of my parents made sure I had a strong work ethic so that I would be tough enough to meet the difficult times ahead.

My parents were also not afraid to fight for me if they thought my rights were being abused or disregarded. As a condition upon his taking the job as head priest at Grace Episcopal Church in Manchester, my dad made sure the City of Manchester would accommodate me in a public school or else pay to send me to a private institution. They did not want me placed in a special school for the disabled, which was permissible thirty years ago. The Manchester Central School District was one of the largest in the state, and they were afraid I might get trampled or injured with so many students. They also didn't want to take the necessary steps to conform to my disability and decided it would be cheaper for them to send me to a smaller private school. For the next six years (grades seven through twelve), the City of Manchester paid my private tuition to attend the Derryfield School, one of the top prep schools in New England. I hit the education jackpot.

I received a great education my parents could have never afforded, but it came with a heavy toll—on me! I went from a public school in Greene where they were not sure what to expect of me to a private institution that would challenge me to become a more productive, responsible person. I couldn't fall through the cracks at Derryfield. There were only three hundred students in the entire school, which meant I received a lot of personal attention from my teachers. And I was among the very best and brightest of students. Kids from Derryfield didn't go on to community college; they went to Harvard, Yale, Dartmouth, and Bucknell. They became doctors, lawyers, and leading scientists. There was a tremendous passion for learning, and for that you needed equal parts hard work and intelligence.

My first two-plus years at Derryfield were a real struggle because I wasn't mentally prepared for the amount of work I had to do. I didn't feel as if I fitted in academically with the other students, and therefore I didn't see any reason to bust my butt and try to keep up. I was lazy. It wasn't until my sophomore year that I began to see things differently. I was averaging 100 percent in geometry class, and my teacher, Dennis Holland, took notice. He pulled me aside one afternoon and said, "John, I didn't realize you were so smart!" He was surprised at my grades because up until that point, I hadn't shown I could do such good work. Another of my math teachers, Edward Lemire in algebra, told me much the same, which was basically, "Keep up the good work." I was encouraged by what they said, but it wasn't until my history teacher, Bruce Berk, praised my work that I began to feel as if I belonged at Derryfield and that maybe college was in my future, too. History wasn't something I was very interested in, whereas math was. I had been solving problems—from how to eat with a knife and fork to how to type or reach a high light switch—practically from the day I was born, so it only seemed natural that I'd take a liking to math. But to see that I could get the job done in another curriculum, which wasn't of great interest to me, was huge!

One of the best things prep school did was overload me with schoolwork. When I met up with Mr. Berk in Manchester in 2008, he told me that the teachers strove to get us "eight hours of homework per night," much more than they hand out today. He said their thinking was to give us more than we could handle so that we would have to prioritize what needed to be done, and when. I couldn't possibly do eight hours of homework per night, so I had to determine which work was absolutely necessary to help me get through the next day, then catch up on the rest later. If I had a test in algebra the next day, I made sure to study algebra that night; the ten chapters I had to read for history could wait, since the written exam on it wouldn't take place until the following week. It was all about prioritizing, which proved vital to my success later on at Syracuse University because I knew how much time I needed to set aside every night to study and what I needed to study to keep my grades up. Those final two and a half years at Derryfield prepared me for real life more than anything else, because you had to figure out pretty quickly what's the most important thing you can do "right now."

In TV sales and business, there are enough projects out there to keep me busy twenty-four hours a day. But it's deciding what projects are important and finding solutions to these projects in a timely manner that help set me apart from other salespeople. There are always clients I could call on in person, paperwork I could file, or thank-you notes I could write. It is very easy to get bogged down in tasks that are not essential to completing the overall goal. It is a matter of whether you are just trying to look busy versus really trying to accomplish something.

Here is how I have used that education at Derryfield (and later Syracuse) in my sales career. The adaptation and prioritization of tasks come together in my business calls for the PBS station I work for in Albany. I can call fifteen companies and leave messages in the same amount of time it takes most salespeople to visit two new clients in person. I can e-mail prospects new information in multitude rather than taking a whole day to visit them all individually. This efficiency helps me when I do finally sit down with the client in person. If I am in front of the client and have set an appointment with him or her, then I know that the client thinks the meeting is important. We are there to do business.

In prep school, I also learned that I was better prepared to work on projects I enjoyed rather than ones I did not. Geometry, computer programming, and English literature were more interesting to me than French or chemistry. In college I chose to major in television, radio, and film because I liked the subject matter. In sales I perform better with products I believe in. I work in broadcast television because I believe television advertising works best for clients.

The subject matter has given me an advantage over many other salespeople who have not thought about television or whether it works for their clients. Such an individual is referred to as "the accidental salesperson" by one respected sales trainer I know. It represents most people in media sales who do not seek out a career in media but are employed selling ads. Well, I smile at this thought. My love for broadcasting led me to television sales. It has given me that same advantage I had in high school when I took mostly math and English classes. Because I enjoy the product, it allows me the time to be the salesperson I want to be! I am a consultant, not a peddler.

5

STAND UP AND BE SEEN

MOST HIGH SCHOOL SENIORS receive word of their future college destination via the mail, usually in the form of a very large envelope. I was pulled out of assembly and told I had been accepted to Syracuse University. I'm sure my dad's cousin Daniel Willett, who was an administrator at Syracuse at the time, had something to do with the phone call, because it was no secret in my family how badly I wanted to attend Syracuse. My mom's family was from nearby LaFayette, my uncle Douglas went to SU, and like anyone who grew up in central New York, I bled Orange basketball and football. It didn't hurt that SU had one of the best communications schools in the country, either, because I knew early on that I wanted to pursue a career in television.

I coveted Syracuse for all of those reasons, and because it's a large school. I didn't seek out a small, intimate campus; I wanted a place that would push and prepare me for the real world, not one that would continue to accommodate my disability. In high school my classes were moved to one floor, when possible, so I wouldn't have to walk the stairs, someone carried my books from class to class, and the assistant headmaster assisted me in the bathroom. I

13. My uncle Douglas Morris and I are blowing bubbles in the dining room in my maternal grandparents' home in LaFayette.

was pampered. I needed to be challenged by my new surroundings, because certainly the real world wasn't going to be as obliging. For this reason, I couldn't wait to get to Syracuse and gain my independence. I was dependent on others for so long—for eating, getting dressed, going to the bathroom—and I didn't want to live that way anymore. I frequently asked for help, but I hated to do so. Syracuse was my opportunity to stand alone and see if I could make it on my own.

My independence came with a price, though. That summer I took a job as a telemarketer to raise some cash for school, but, unfortunately, all that money went toward replacing the timing chain that gave out on my mom's 1982 Chevy Citation—the car my future roommates would later dub "The Silver Bullet." So I didn't have much cash for incidentals or for entertainment when I first arrived on campus, but I did have a vehicle. The car would solve the problem of how I'd get from one class to another.

My next biggest dilemma that summer was making sure I could dress myself for every situation. In Syracuse, that means one thing in particular—snow! Up until then, I relied on my parents and others to dress me. I couldn't button my pants, or fasten a tie. Fortunately, a friend of my mom's, Nancy Fischer, figured out a way to use a Velcro strap instead of a button to secure my pants. Through much trial and error, Nancy attached a long piece of Velcro to my pants that I could pull through the buttonhole and fasten to the waistband. Voilà! Problem solved.

Many more questions awaited answers when I arrived up on the Hill in late August 1986. Would I be able to get to my classes on time? How would I get my food? My tray? Would I find parking close to my classrooms? What if I'm unable to reach the elevator buttons? How am I going to carry my books without taking a nosedive? The first few weeks were like an episode of *The Amazing Race*. There were challenges at seemingly every turn, but I took them on one at a time. First, I wanted to see if I could get through a full day, then a week, then my first test, and so on. With each passing day, I gained more and more confidence in myself that I could survive on my own.

My biggest physical challenge was getting around from class to class. That first semester, I *lost* fifteen pounds. While most first-year students were packing on the "freshman fifteen," I was shedding pounds like a wrestler trying to make weight. In the Hall of Languages, one of the older buildings on campus where I had classes, I couldn't reach the buttons on the elevator so I had to walk up and down several flights of stairs; it was either that or wait for someone else who could reach the buttons. There were stairs everywhere, not to mention one steep hill I had to navigate from the Hall of Languages to the Schine Student Center, where I worked part-time at the student organization desk. When there was snow or ice on the sidewalks and steps, things got a bit tricky.

My parents were petrified of my going to school. Mom called me every morning at seven thirty that first semester just to check up on me; Dad called me once a week. I'm sure it was hard on them at first because they weren't sure I'd be able to adapt to my new surroundings, just as I wasn't. At the same time, they were ready for me to move on. They knew I wouldn't be happy if I stayed at home forever.

The first few weeks would answer the questions I had as to whether I could get around and exist on my own. I could. But I still hadn't addressed my other great fear, which was whether I could make new friends. It was very difficult at first. I had been spoiled by a high school, church, and family that provided me special treatment, and here was a new group of people not ready to hand me friendship because I asked for it. I had to earn it.

I was not the center of attention at Syracuse, as I was in high school or at home. I had to find my way to class and stand in line for the dining hall just like every other student. For the first time, I felt like I stood on merit with my peers. But I was still different. I was so busy trying to figure out who I was that I did not realize the other students needed a transition period to get used to me. Not everyone is excited to welcome someone with differences into their own lives. I had made a few friends in my dormitory with whom I shared things in common, but others were still very leery of me.

I lived on the first floor of Sadler Hall my freshman and sophomore years at SU. The dormitory was right across the street from the Carrier Dome, which was ideal for me because I could leave fifteen minutes before the opening kickoff or tip-off and still make it to my seat on time. It also had a very large field in the back adjacent to Lawrinson Hall, which students turned into a beach on those rare warm, sunny days in the spring. It was also used for intramural softball and touch football games, as well as the occasional mud or tackle football game, which almost led to my demise. I'll get into that story shortly.

My roommate freshman year hailed from northern California. Roberto and I spoke on the phone a month before I arrived on campus, which is a common occurrence with most incoming freshmen. But I did not tell Roberto of my physical disability, and when he walked in the door his first day at Syracuse he was caught off guard.

Roberto put on a good face for the first few days as my roommate, but then spent more and more time in another dorm. Not long after freshman orientation, Roberto came to the room and said he was uncomfortable living with me. He wanted to transfer to a new dorm. I was rejected two weeks into my college life.

I was very upset. I expected to have a roommate and a new friend, as all incoming freshmen do; instead, I was living in my own bedroom, and I didn't know a soul. I spent a lot of time exploring campus, driving my car, working in the student center, and studying. I can remember writing a letter to a friend from high school, telling her about Roberto's rejection and how I couldn't understand why someone would feel that uncomfortable around me. She told me to forget about it. "That's his loss, not yours," she said.

One positive that came out of Roberto's departure was that I had my own room. I was the envy of every freshman in Sadler because I had some freedom other kids weren't able to have—and my own bathroom. This freedom eventually allowed me to find new friends.

I struck up several friendships with my neighbors on the West Wing of Sadler 1. Jivi Govender lived across the hall along with Yardley Drake Buckman. For some reason Yardley, who hailed from Florida, didn't know how cold it got in Syracuse, and he brought only a light jacket with him. He stuck it out for a long time with that jacket, too. Jivi was Indian by way of South Africa and was raised in a small town next to Greene, where I lived until the seventh grade. We shared some acquaintances. We'd stay up late, listen to music, and talk about girls. When relatives called him, he would hold the phone up to my ear so I could hear the accents from South Africa. We had a great freshman year getting to know each other and would share a dorm suite our junior year with two other friends, both of whom lived on Sadler 1 our freshman year.

That September Jivi's family bought a golf course near Syracuse. It was a huge perk to be able to play there as a student. When we graduated from Syracuse, Jivi made me a lifetime member of Camillus Country Club. It was a tremendous gift. I didn't view it as an offer to play golf as much as a request that we stay close friends and remain in each other's lives, and we have.

My next-door neighbors were both recruited to play soccer at Syracuse—Stefan Sandkuhl, an exchange student from Germany, and Craig Hubmeier, a big New York Rangers fan from Long Island. We talked a lot of hockey. I shared trips to the dining hall with him and Stefan, and they shared trips in my car. The three of us along with Jivi and Yardley took a trip to New York City in my car early that November. It was quite a trip, up until the time I got pulled over by the NYPD on Forty-second Street for making an illegal right-hand turn. The officer was not too happy, but there are some advantages to being physically disabled, and one of them is that you frequently get pardoned by the cops. He had also pulled a taxicab over behind me for the same violation, and he was giving the driver no slack. He chewed him out pretty good. The rest of the time we spent sightseeing. We also visited Craig's parents on Long Island.

I was making friends—new friends—in part because of what my disability provided me: I had a car. I was okay with it. My father would tell me, "Good friends provide what is missing for each other—a give-and-take relationship." I didn't feel used at all. It's not taking advantage of someone if both parties are happy with the arrangement. They were happy I could give them an occasional lift to class, and I was grateful for their company.

Craig and I often headed to the Sheraton on campus and watched hockey in the lounge. It didn't matter if his Rangers or my Boston Bruins were on TV; we shared a passion for the game, and it was great fun to hang out with him. We'd eat peanuts and popcorn and buy just enough beer with what little money we had so they wouldn't throw us out. He and I were a lot alike—stubborn, opinionated, and very determined. But the thing I valued most about Craig was that he didn't treat me like a charity case; he picked on me just as he would anyone else. In fact, one time he duct-taped my walking cane to the ceiling in my room so I couldn't reach it. Although I didn't think it was funny at the time, it was just the balance I was looking for.

My first impression of the students who lived on the other wing of Sadler 1 was that they were very loud. I didn't know if they were going to like me or not, but I could envision having a lot of fun with those guys. They were all instant friends, and I was trying to make an impression to gain their attention. It turned out to be a big mistake: I didn't realize if I was myself they would like me; that awareness would come later. One day I stupidly opened my mouth and challenged the guys on Sadler

2 to a game of tackle football. The loser had to buy the winning floor a half-keg of beer. Although we had some good athletes on our floor, we were much better drinkers than we were football players. And Sadler 2 boasted some pretty big dudes. I arranged the game and then informed the guys only after the game had started that our money was on the line. We lost, and my floor mates were angry, and rightfully so. I was looking for a way to be included and found a way to alienate all of those guys instead. I was not acting like myself. I was being obnoxious, hoping to be noticed.

I started to spend more time on the other side of the floor during the second semester, but it wasn't until the April Block Party in Walnut Park that I began to feel accepted by the other guys. The Red Hot Chili Peppers headlined the party, and the entire afternoon people were curious enough to hang around me and get to know me better. I remember after the party eating in the dining hall alone with one of the guys from the West Wing, Dave Allen (who just happened to be the quarterback on the losing side), because everyone else had passed out. We wound up talking for hours that night and remain very close friends today. Dave, in fact, is the godfather of my daughter, Ariel.

In my second year at Syracuse, I started to become more comfortable. I was less worried about who liked me and for what reason. I had a great friendship with Craig, who had moved to the seventh floor at Sadler, and did not need to try as hard to be noticed. Most of the other guys from Sadler 1 during freshman year, whom I had alienated by acting like a jerk, lived just across the street at Stadium Place. The guys asked if Craig and I would like to join a fantasy baseball league, and we gladly accepted, which helped bring us all a lot closer.

My single room, held over from freshman year, soon became one of our meeting places, but not so much for the league as for the cable TV box that was installed at the start of the semester. Sadler was one of the first dorms

14. A first reunion of sorts among college friends in the fall of 1991. The occasion was to transfer the very important Orange League (our college fantasy baseball league) trophy to the new champions, Robert Aronow and Scott Roegiers *(back row, left to right)*. Craig Hubmeier and I are in the front row.

to get hooked up (Stadium wasn't so lucky), so my room was suddenly as popular a destination as the bars on Marshall Street. Paul Golden, who managed the snack bar at Sadler, visited frequently, as did Craig, Dave, and three other Stadium guys, Rob Aronow, Scott Roegiers, and Pat Kelleher. Rob would watch anything. He and Paul were there so much, you'd think it was their room. We watched a lot of baseball, basketball, and, of course, hockey—especially at play-off time.

Although my new friends helped me acclimate to life as a student, there were still times my disability was projected back to me like a mirror. One night Craig, Dave, and I were filing out of a nightclub called Braggs. Craig is six-foot-one and Dave six-foot-three, so I was a

15. With my college friends at Patrick Kelleher's wedding in 1996. *Back row, left to right:* Paul Golden, Robert Aronow, Pat, and Scott Roegiers. *Front row:* Dave Allen and me.

sight standing between the two of them. The place was packed with people—I'm sure they broke every fire code in Syracuse—and it was slow getting out of there. The bouncer wouldn't let anybody into the club until a certain number of people left, and the people waiting in line were getting restless. Suddenly, one woman in line looked down at me (she had probably had a few too many already) and yelled for everyone to hear, "If you'd just get off your knees, this line would move a lot faster!" Well, my two friends thought that was the funniest thing they had ever heard and laughed hysterically. They couldn't wait to get back and tell everyone what they heard.

It's never fun to be laughed at, but having found new friends who understood me far outweighed any discomfort I may have felt by the woman's insulting me. The person I was in high school would have dwelled on the fact that someone saw me as a person with a disability first. It took many days and nights of reflection to realize that what's important are the friends I have made, not the people who stare at me.

There were many times in high school when I chose not to push myself, because I didn't have the self-confidence I would later exude at Syracuse. It was very difficult to grow up with forty brothers and sisters in such a small graduating class at prep school because there was no need to challenge myself or test new relationships. I felt as if I were in some tiny, sheltered cocoon. I am thankful every day for that education, but it's the life skills I received at Syracuse University that truly made me the person I am today.

First and foremost among those life skills was the self-confidence I gained by proving to myself that I could be independent. I may choose to have other people help me from time to time, but I don't need anyone else to live. I learned to adapt to situations I was shielded from prior to college, which improved my mobility and problem-solving skills. I chose to work hard. It's what my parents wanted for me, and it's what I wanted for myself. I always wanted to have a family, a nice car, and a dream home, but it wasn't until I stood on my own and got off my knees that I realized I could achieve those things.

To me, getting off my knees means hard work. I tell myself I need to work twice as hard to climb up in a chair, to buy groceries, to dress my children. It takes me twenty-five minutes to get my son Owen into his hockey gear. And then I have to ask someone else to help him with his skates. How long does it take you to dress your child? I need to push myself. This mind-set is what I use every day. If I tell myself I need to work twice as hard to be the equal of others, then I will.

6

Fueling My
Competitive Drive

LIKE ANY FIRST-TIME PARENT, my father had a mental image of what his son or daughter would look like, what he or she would be growing up, and what they'd accomplish. If he had a boy, he'd want him to be more athletic and competitive than he was. My father was not interested in sports. He enjoyed music—he played the organ, piano, and trombone—and singing. He also liked to play poker, hunt, and fish. And although he did take up golf when we moved to Greene, New York, it was mainly so he could spend time with the other community and church leaders in the town.

You can only imagine his disappointment upon first glimpse of his newborn son, a congenital amputee with no arms below the elbows and no knees. His shock and grief were mixed with feelings of anger and hopelessness, for many of the dreams and expectations that he and my mom had for me had instantly vanished. Or so they thought. Certainly, I was never going to be able to swing a golf club like Jack Nicklaus, or wield a bat like Mickey Mantle, or play the trombone. In the first few

16. My father, David, fishing on Lake Winnipesaukee in New Hampshire on a summer vacation in the mid-1990s.

days after my birth, it was uncertain whether I'd ever be able to walk on my own.

As time wore on, however, and my parents became more acquainted with me and what I could or couldn't do physically, they discovered that I was capable of doing many things, and that included playing sports. My mother, because she grew up on a farm just six miles outside of Syracuse, was a big fan of Syracuse football and basketball, and would catch as many of their games on television as she could. Every Saturday afternoon in the fall you knew exactly where to find her, and that was in the TV room. I was right beside her, and it wasn't long before I was mimicking the athletes I saw on TV around the house. I had a garbage can in my room that I turned into a makeshift basketball hoop, and I would shoot my Nerf ball into the basket. I also had a Nerf football that I liked to toss up in the air to myself, often at the expense of the couch that frequently served as the line of scrimmage or the goal line.

My parents were happy to see that I had such a strong passion for sports and were pleasantly surprised by the agility I showed in playing ball around the house. My dad recognized it early, and decided to take me to the golf course with him to see if I might have an interest in the game. Naturally, I couldn't wait to get my arms around the clubs. At seven, I wasn't strong enough to hit the ball in the air, but I could putt. I'd wedge the handle of my dad's flat-bladed putter under both of my armpits, and swing the putter on the large carpet we had downstairs. One Christmas, Dad bought me an electronic putter return. It was one of those machines that returned the ball to you even if you missed the hole by an inch or two (I like to think that's why I'm always two balls outside the cup on my misses now). I'd putt for hours at a time, seeing if I could make two in a row, then five, then ten.

I would have to turn the putter around, however, and putt with the toe of the blade because I was left-handed. I found that I could make a longer, freer swing as a lefty than I could as a righty.

The first club my dad bought for me was a knock-off left-handed 7-iron that he had cut down for me, so it wasn't too long or heavy to swing. I'd hit plastic balls all over the yard, saving the real balls for when I played at my grandparents' farm in LaFayette. It had a lot more real estate and margin for error—not to mention fewer windows—should I badly miss my target.

I spent a great deal of my summers as a child at my grandparents' farm playing golf and baseball. When my granddad was out working in the fields, I'd take the 7-iron out and whack balls around the yard. I had built a make-shift five-hole course on the property, using tuna cans to fill in for holes I cut into the ground. Each golf hole measured approximately a hundred feet, or about thirty to thirty-five yards long, and I'd make my way around the course with my 7-iron and putter, holing out with my putter each time I got within several feet of the cans. As I got older and started to mow the lawn, I refined the course a bit, cutting the grass lower in spots to create the appearance of closely mown fairways and greens. It wasn't Augusta National or Pebble Beach Golf Links, but in my imagination it was.

I would also tag along with my uncle Douglas and his friend Charlie Petrie during their Friday-afternoon rounds at Skaneateles Greens. At first, I only drove the cart, but before long I was playing all nine holes with them. My uncle sprayed the ball around everywhere, which didn't serve him well. I realized fairly quickly that if I could hit the ball straight and keep it in play, I could take advantage of the hard, fast fairways and get more roll and distance from my shots. Because my swing wasn't very long or very fast, it wasn't hard to hit it straight, and I found I could hold my own against Uncle Douglas and Charlie.

Not long after I started playing golf, my father got us tickets to see the B.C. Open in nearby Endicott, New York. It was at this men's PGA Tour event that I had my first brush with a professional athlete. My father and I liked to camp out by the sixteenth and eighteenth greens, and lo and behold one day Chi Chi Rodriguez stopped by to say hi to me. I think a tournament official or Chi Chi's

17. On the campus of Beloit College in Wisconsin with my uncle Douglas Morris.

caddie alerted him to where I was standing, but he signed a ball for me and also gave us two tickets to the next two rounds of the tournament. So we wound up going on Saturday and Sunday: Chi Chi tipped his hat to me every time he saw me, and I now had a favorite golfer—until another lefty, Phil Mickelson, came on the scene about a dozen years later.

Shortly after we moved to Manchester, New Hampshire, my parents bought me my first set of real golf clubs. The set included a Wilson driver, 3-wood, 7-iron, and putter. Not coincidentally, these four clubs are what I use most often today. I like the 3-wood because it launches the ball in the air easily, and the 7-iron is a club I'm extremely comfortable with because I've hit it thousands of times. A local pro and club fitter in nearby Voorheesville, New York, Frank Mellet, builds most of my clubs now, and my set includes a few more irons as well as the latest in rocket-launching technology: I have a Ping G10 driver and several hybrids.

Like most other challenges I've confronted in my life, learning how to play golf took some trial and error, and some study. I watched professional golfers on TV and realized that in order to hit the ball, I had to swing the club back and through on a large, pendulum-like arc. As I did with baseball, I held the club under my right armpit and swung my right arm toward the ball. The easiest way to describe my swing is that the club is an extension of my right arm. It's a one-lever swing, and I create my power by bringing the clubhead back some, and then turning my chest and body through toward the target as hard as I can. My left arm pushes the club a little bit, but all it's really doing is guiding it. To this day, people are amazed that I can hit the ball as far and accurately as I do, but I still occasionally tinker with the idea of playing with a prosthetic arm that will allow me to create more clubhead speed. Why not? Who isn't looking for extra distance off the tee?

It's that feeling of competitiveness, of striving to be better, that I love most about golf. Thanks to the U.S. Golf Association's handicap system, I'm able to compete against other golfers on a fairly even playing ground, because I'm getting an extra stroke or two per hole. It's the most accommodating sport there is because of the handicap system, and because there are different sets of tees you can play from that make the hole play shorter in length based on your skill level. Golf is designed for someone who's eight years old, thirty-eight, or eighty. You can fit the course to the ability of the player, and that's why I like it. It feeds into my independent nature, too. My whole life has been about standing on my own, and with golf I can go out there with three other guys, no matter what they look like or what their skill level is, and compete against them.

Or I can go out alone. I enjoy the occasional solitude golf provides, like when I'm standing by myself on the fifth and twelfth tees at Camillus Country Club, high above the fairway, looking around at the surrounding holes and countryside. It's so peaceful, a great release from

18. Paul Golden *(left)*, Robert Aronow *(right)*, and
I meet for a round of golf in 2003.

the stresses of work and everyday life. I frequently played
alone when I was working in Syracuse. It was nice to have
no clients around, just me, my golf ball, and nature. That's
not to say I don't like company on the course. One of the
best things about golf is the camaraderie you feel among

friends and the lasting friendships you make as a result of the game. My favorite annual event is the Camillus Country Club Member-Guest Tournament, which takes place the third weekend in July. For three days, you get to play *a lot* of golf, which is a compelling-enough reason to make the two-and-a-half-hour journey west to the Syracuse suburbs. But I also get the chance to tee it up with my playing partner, Dave Allen (the ghostwriter on this book), and two of my other closest friends from my Syracuse University days, Rob Aronow and Jivi Govender. I also frequently get to play with people I've never met or had only a nodding acquaintance with over the years. It's a bit nerve-wracking in the beginning being pitted against somebody new, but after a few holes it's as if we've played together for years. The awkwardness disappears once they see I can really play, and after I've had a beer or two with them. It's ironic, but many of the groups who are initially frightened or uncomfortable playing with Dave and me request that they be paired with us the following year.

Each year Dave and I joke about how we're going to shock the world at this tournament and win our flight. But each year since we began playing in this event in the mid-1990s, we've finished last or second to last in the final flight. Dave kids me about how much his shoulders hurt from carrying me all the time, but I've had my share of moments where I've picked him up, like the one year I made par on the par-five sixteenth hole, one of my most thrilling memories in golf. What made it even better is that my wife, Andrea, and one of our Syracuse classmates,

Paul Golden, were there to witness it and catch it on video-tape. I've also been a steady contributor on the par-threes over the years, but as teammates, Dave and I are not the best at ham-and-egging it. I know our poor performances eat at Dave, who's been a writer in the golf business since 1997, but we both have a tremendous amount of fun, and hardly a phone discussion passes without one of us bringing up the Member-Guest.

I mentioned the par I had above in the Member-Guest, but my favorite golf memory, maybe my sports highlight, has to be when I made a birdie on the par-three 124-yard seventh hole at Tralee Golf Club in Ireland. I hit my tee shot pin high on the right side of the green, but the hole was cut to the left on a lower tier. Somehow I managed to nestle the downhill 25-foot breaking putt into the hole. I have to believe that God was looking after me on that putt, because when you're playing golf in Ireland, you are in God's country. It's hard to imagine a more spectacular setting. Tralee sits on a peninsula on the rugged south-western coast of Ireland, with views of the Atlantic Ocean from nearly every hole. It was the first European course designed by Arnold Palmer, and one of his favorites. Said Palmer of the links-style venue widely considered one of the best ocean courses in the world, "I may have designed the front nine, but surely God designed the back nine."

Tralee was the second of three courses that Dave and I visited on a golf vacation to Ireland in August 2007. Dave had spent the prior week in Scotland reporting on the Women's British Open. We met up in Ireland and stayed in the town of Doonbeg for the first few days, which was home to another fabulous links course, Doonbeg Golf Course, where we played on our second day in Ireland. Tralee followed, and then we concluded our short trip with a round at Ballybunion Golf Club. Unfortunately, we couldn't get a tee time at the Old Course there, but we did play the Cashen Course, which was designed by famous golf-course architect Robert Trent Jones Sr. This was probably the most difficult of the three courses we played that week, and not because of the sloping terrain and sand dunes that engulfed each fairway but because of the weather. Finally, we had rain—a lot of it—and it proved most challenging as we tried to navigate our buggy (what they call a golf cart in Ireland) up and down the slick, rolling hills at Ballybunion. Because of my disability, we were allowed to use a buggy. We were the only ones riding a buggy that day and with good reason: the rain caused the wheels to lock up at the top of one roller coaster of a fairway, causing the cart to spin 360 degrees and then skid down the hill backward at about 30 mph. Yes, backward! Dave said he nearly jumped out, and the thought crossed my mind at one point, too. Had either of us done so, I think the cart would have flipped over with the other one still in it. It wasn't so funny at the time, but after our hearts had a chance to travel back down from our throats, we were laughing hysterically.

That near-fatal buggy ride, the 203-yard drive I hit earlier that round at Ballybunion (my longest ever), the birdie at Tralee, and the walk among the tall, grassy dunes at Doonbeg are memories that I will cherish for a lifetime. But not one of them would've happened if my parents

19. Here I am preparing to hit my first tee shot at Doonbeg Golf Club in Ireland in August 2007. My drive traveled 125 yards and came to rest just off the fairway, in the right rough.

hadn't encouraged me to pursue my love of sports and if I had accepted the traditional thinking that people with disabilities aren't supposed to play sports. I can't imagine what my life would be without sports. At first it was a way to make friends, and to feel normal. When I was outside playing Wiffle ball or basketball out in the drive-way with the other neighborhood kids, I wasn't thinking about my physical disability. I was playing and having fun. As I got older and I could no longer compete on the same level with the other boys at sports like basketball and football, I became a fan and began a love affair that continues today with sports franchises such as the Boston Bruins, Pittsburgh Steelers, and New York Yankees.

While the Yankees and Steelers have spoiled me with so many championship moments, it is the Bruins whom I most identify with—and, you might say, suffer with. When we moved to New Hampshire days after my twelfth birthday, I was already hooked on the sport. Just ten months earlier, the U.S. hockey team pulled off the "Miracle on Ice" and defeated the Russians at the Winter Olympic Games in Lake Placid. Jim Craig, the goalten-der and face of that U.S. team, was now tending the net for the Bruins, which made it that much more exciting to catch their games on TV. The Montreal Canadiens also received a lot of airtime because there was a large contin-gent of French Canadians living in the Manchester area, so I'd watch their games, too. In high school I served as the manager of the hockey team, logging the score book and helping out with the equipment as best I could. I was another set of eyes on the bench to make sure that we had the correct number of players on the ice and the right match-ups. I could never skate and play, but being so close to the action was like being out on the ice for real.

Sports have enriched my life and provided me with so many great memories over the years that I can honestly say to my father now that his wish for me did come true. God may not have blessed me with an athletic body, but he did provide me with an intense passion for sports, one I share today with my children and closest friends. My oldest son, Haydon, and I have a common interest in sports, especially football. We attended Super Bowl XL between the Steelers and Seattle Seahawks in February 2006 in Detroit, which is my all-time favorite sports memory. My youngest boy, Owen, has started to play hockey, and my daughter, Ariel, dreams one day of being an Olympic swimmer.

Having a rooting interest in a favorite team or individual is another way for me to feel normal, like everyone else. It has given me something to cheer about and discuss with my friends and children. It's something we can all share and care about, love and hate, or argue about. It provides hope in times of despair and can lift a whole city, state, or even country, as the U.S. hockey team proved in 1980. Anyone can compete in sports provided they've got a mind and some mobility. If, like me, you're an amputee, there is adaptive equipment out there to help you ski, play golf, or run. If you're a paraplegic, there are wheelchair basketball and football leagues out there for you to enjoy. Yes, you're limited to some extent, but there are outlets to help you fuel that competitive streak. Don't let anyone ever tell you that you can't play and compete.

7

Turning Obstacles
into Opportunities

ONE CHALLENGE that is difficult for me is describing to a potential client how I look. "I stand only three feet nine inches tall. I was born without my arms (including hands) from the elbows down. My legs formed without my upper thighs and corresponding bone structure, so my hips are attached to my lower legs. I do not have knees, and I walk in a shuffling motion." Imagine being on the other end of the line and hearing that I'm the person you're going to meet with in less than twenty-four hours! Then imagine you are me and you have to explain it to somebody.

First impressions (more on this subject in the next chapter) are just one of the many everyday obstacles I've had to overcome in trying to fit myself into an able-bodied world. Others include:

• accepting the idea that I will always be much shorter in a taller world;

• reaching items up high, from light switches to shelves to the microwave oven;

• learning how to use computer keyboards, a cell phone, and other devices that require fingers;

- driving a vehicle when my feet can't reach the floor and my arms can't grasp the steering wheel.

Being born without extensions to my arms and legs provided me with what most people would perceive to be an insurmountable obstacle; it would be understandable if I took a mulligan and stayed at home on my couch collecting Social Security. For a while I felt this way, too, but now I'm blessed to see these obstacles before me as opportunities. When I see a challenge ahead I take the time to think about it, and then I come up with a solution. I don't see these obstacles as dead ends ("No, I can't type"; "No, I'll never learn how to drive a car"); rather, I see them as opportunities for growth and a chance to better my life. If I can figure out a way to overcome these challenges, then I'm no longer burdened by what I perceive to be a problem, and I'm a much happier person for it.

Everyone reading this book feels saddled by something that causes them stress. Think about it: There is something weighing heavily on you. It could be that you're worried about the test you have next week, or the credit card bills you have to pay. It could be a first date, or an upcoming job interview. It may be that your job is in jeopardy, or that you just accepted a new job and you have two weeks to pack your belongings and move from New York City to Los Angeles. You've got all of these challenges in your head that you're building up as obstacles against some sort of happiness—your personal happiness! Instead of thinking of these things as obstacles, think about the opportunities they provide and how happy you'll be when you do succeed.

It's as much about having a positive attitude as anything else, and believing how much stronger and relieved you'll be when you've come up with a solution to your problem. Take the example of the person above who is relocating for their new job. Instead of looking at things in a negative light or worrying himself to death (Should I rent a truck and drive out or hire movers? How am I going to get everything out of my apartment? Can I afford a one- or two-bedroom in Los Angeles? What neighborhoods should I be looking in? Will my landlord let me out of my current lease? What do I do about transportation when I get to California?), he should be thinking about how lucky he is to have this opportunity when many people today are out of work and struggling to make ends meet. He should be excited about leaving the cold and snow behind for the sunshine, beaches, and year-round golf season he will soon get to enjoy.

Let me give you a few examples of obstacles I have confronted in my life and how I was able to turn them into opportunities. First and foremost, there was teaching myself how to dress. To this day, I believe that this simple act was my greatest life achievement. Yes, I have broken a hundred on the golf course, I'm married, and I have fathered two beautiful children and raised a stepson; I can change a diaper, shave, pump my own gas, text someone on my cell phone, and throw a football. But nothing has helped my individual self-esteem and business career more than learning how to button and zipper a pair of pants and knot my own tie.

When I was a seventeen-year-old senior at prep school in Manchester, I wasn't thinking only about college applications, finals, and girls; I was also worrying about how I was going to dress myself on my own when I did go off to college in September. In grammar school it wasn't much of a concern to me. At home my parents and sister provided help, and at school it was the principal or school nurse who helped me dress and undress and go to the bathroom. In gym class I wore the clothes I already had on instead of changing. I did my best to avoid situations where I needed to ask new people to help me dress. For example, I did not stay overnight at other kids' homes but asked if they could stay with us.

As I got older I was able to pull on a T-shirt and my underwear and pants with the help of a wooden cane, but I was still unable to button my pants or put on my socks. I hated asking people for assistance even if they were good friends and didn't mind helping me. It was a limiting feeling, and a burden I had to overcome in my own mind. I needed to be seen as an independent person, and I couldn't do that if I required help every time I had to button my pants or go to the bathroom. I wanted to attend college away from home, but I had this giant weight on my shoulders that I had to drop first. I had to solve this problem of dressing myself. Then along came a family friend, and a major obstacle soon became an enormous opportunity.

Several months before I was to leave for my freshman year at Syracuse University, I had a brainstorming session with Nancy Fischer, who had done some tailoring for me in the past. The big question was how we could fix the button on my pants so I'd be able to undo and fasten it on my own. We thought about a snap button, but then I'd have the same problem: I wouldn't be able to reach it. A string? I couldn't tie it. Velcro? Aha! Now we were on to something. Nancy took two one-inch pieces of Velcro and attached them to either side of the pants where the button was, and then I put the pants on. Unfortunately, the Velcro wasn't strong enough to hold. Next, she took a six-and-a-half-inch strip of Velcro and sewed it to the outside of the waistband to the right of where the button was, and attached another piece of the same length to the opposite side, leaving most of it unsewed and dangling. With the help of a shoelace she attached to the end of the unsewed strip, I was then able to thread it through the buttonhole, pull tight, and fasten to the waistband—much like a belt goes through a belt buckle. It worked!

Now all we had to do was find a way to pull up the zipper. A similar loop of shoelace was attached to the zipper, and with the aid of a cut-down curtain rod I would essentially use as a finger, I was able to dress myself for the first time. I felt so proud. As long as I was prepared, I could now dress and undress myself every day. When I arrived at college that fall, no one was the wiser of my inventions. Most important, I was completely independent.

I learned something about myself that summer: if there's a will, there's a way. I could figure out solutions to my problems through much trial and error. They may not turn out as I imagined, but if I am open-minded and relentless in my pursuit, there are solutions.

Once I learned to tighten my pants, the next big challenge would be learning how to tie my own tie. This task wasn't a necessity for me in college, so I didn't tackle it until I was several years into my sales career. In the spring of 2000 I took a new job as a regional account executive with WNYT-NBC13 in Albany. My family remained in Syracuse for several months, so until they were able to join me my wife, Andrea, set me up with five dress shirts and ties, all pretied, for the week. One week, however, I made the mistake of leaving Syracuse with only the shirts and no ties. Once I realized it, a sense of panic overtook me. It was as if I had locked myself out of the house and the keys were nowhere to be found. I was desperate. I had to either find a way to knot a necktie on my own or drive five hours round-trip to Syracuse to pick up the ties I had left behind. I even considered calling in sick the next day, but then I realized that here was something I needed to resolve once and for all. I went out to the mall, bought a new tie, and spent several hours that night at my friend Paul's home in front of the mirror learning how to tie my own necktie.

It wasn't easy, but in any problem there is a solution if you're willing to put the time and effort into solving it. First, I placed the tie loosely around the shirt's button-down collar. Then I put the shirt on and fastened all of the buttons using an old button hooker my parents purchased for me when I was a kid. The end on the metal hook slides through the buttonhole and grips the button, making it easy to pull through the hole. Once all of the buttons were secure, the big challenge was figuring out how to bring the end of the tie up through the loop and then down through the knot in front, then tightening it so it looked like a true Windsor knot. The latter part was especially difficult, but I learned I could do it with my mouth.

You would have to see it to believe it, but I practiced this method for hours that night to the point where I almost felt like eating the tie. But I did it, and a big mental hurdle was cleared. Now I didn't have to worry about who I was traveling with or have my ties pretied before leaving on a business trip. I could fly to St. Louis the next day for a meeting and be ready all by myself. Overcoming this obstacle, however small it may appear, allowed me to progress in my business career and gain a measure of confidence I would have never discovered had I not pushed myself.

Of course, if I had to drive to St. Louis, I could do that, too, because driving was yet another difficult obstacle I was able to overcome along the way. It didn't seem like it at the time, but learning how to drive just might have been the single most important part of my independence.

As a kid growing up in Greene, I rode a Big Wheel around the neighborhood because I wasn't able to handle a bike. I also had a skateboard, but I had to lie down on my stomach to ride it. There was little indication I'd be able to drive a car. My big break came as a teenager, when I learned how to drive a riding lawn mower on my grandparents' farm in LaFayette. The brake and gas pedals were on the left side, and I was able to apply pressure to both using an apple basket and stick we attached to my left arm. It worked really well except for the few times I dropped the basket. One time I had to jump from the mower as it hurtled down a large hill toward the road because I had lost the basket and couldn't reach the brakes. My grandparents seemed unfazed, other than how bad the lawn looked when I finished.

When I was sixteen, my father located a drivers education teacher in Jaffrey, New Hampshire, who taught people with disabilities to drive using hand controls. Paul St. Pierre had a big, old used station wagon with controls on the left side of the steering column, similar to where the apple basket was on the riding mower. This setup was perfect for me. The hand controls worked at a

20. At my maternal grandparents' farm in LaFayette, New York. As a teenager, I learned to drive using this lawn mower.

right angle: I put my left arm out and pushed the controls straight ahead to use the brakes and pulled the controls down toward my left thigh for the gas. It seemed simple enough, and it worked.

Now all I had to do was find a way to raise three hundred dollars for my own hand controls, so I would have a car for my freshman year at Syracuse University. It was difficult to part with, but I wound up selling my collection of 1950s baseball cards that a friend of the family had given to me. The set included cards of Mickey Mantle, Yogi Berra, Ted Williams, and Pee Wee Reese, and while none were in mint condition, they were certainly worth more than the money I received for them at the time. It was with that money that I purchased the hand controls. Was it a good bargain? Let's just say I wouldn't be where I am today without being able to drive a car. My mom's 1982 Chevy Citation got me to and from my classes at SU for four years. It was priceless!

Not every obstacle immediately presents itself as an opportunity. It's hard to think that anything good can come out of losing your job or finding yourself in debt, but if you really take the time to analyze your situation and put it in perspective, you have a chance to turn it into something positive. A case in point: Before I landed my first sales job with NBC affiliate WSTM in Syracuse in 1994, I must have gone on more than twenty unsuccessful job interviews. Naturally, I wanted each job, and I was very disappointed when I didn't get any offers. I started to think that no one would hire me because of my physical appearance, even though I was more than qualified to work in television sales. I can remember interviewing at CBC in Toronto for a research job with Canada's national public broadcaster. It didn't pay very much, but it didn't matter: it was the home of *Hockey Night in Canada*!

21. Here I am behind the wheel of my Chevy Citation during my college years at Syracuse University. You can see the hand controls attached to the steering column. The photograph was taken by a classmate as part of a student photo essay for the S. I. Newhouse School of Public Communications.

In the long run, the best situation for me was the one I eventually had with WSTM, because it paid more money and, since I stayed at my grandmother's, allowed me to save for a home. More important, it gave me a chance to prove myself in sales at a time when I had a lot of confidence; I was the top-billing account executive for two years at WSTM. It was hard to view the many rejections I received as something positive at the time, that perhaps those jobs might have been the wrong opportunities for me. But in retrospect, everything happens for a reason, and what surely looked like an obstacle at the time proved to be the best thing for my career.

In today's world the most serious barriers come from within ourselves and the way we face our obstacles. I am referring to both physical as well as mental barriers placed on us by the preconceived notions of others. My physical barrier is that I'm a congenital amputee; the mental barrier is how that is perceived by society in general and whether I choose to accept that perception. People who see me play golf are utterly amazed because they can't believe a guy without full arms and legs can hit a golf ball 150 yards. They assume that anyone in a wheelchair or with a physical disability can't play sports. A lot of people are just as surprised to hear that I'm married and have kids. These barriers are all mental obstacles placed by society's stereotypes that I have had to overcome to be the successful salesman, father, and husband I am today.

Your physical barrier could be that you're too short, obese, or partially paralyzed. You may have suffered a crippling knee injury playing football in college that has you walking today with a pronounced limp. These examples are just some obstacles that people confront on an everyday basis. But does it mean that you should give up on your dreams and take a seat on the couch because that's what society has come to expect of people in your situation? Absolutely not.

People with disabilities today are fortunate to have more accessibility than in the past, which helps to overcome these physical barriers. For example, any multistory building constructed today must install elevators, and the buttons must be reachable for someone at wheelchair height; in addition, schools and businesses have to provide reasonable accommodations for people with disabilities. Society has become more accepting of the differences among people, which has opened more doors and opportunities for people with disabilities—both mental and physical. Yet there are far too many people out there who don't want to take the risk to pursue these opportunities, either because they're afraid of failure or because they're afraid that society will see them as a failure. Too often, they're looking for an excuse or someone or something to blame instead of trying to find a real solution to their problems. People with disabilities need to do all that they can to push themselves to be whoever it is they want to be. They need to take responsibility for the person they are and look for opportunities to succeed.

My first sales manager at WSTM in Syracuse gave me a little sign that read, "Whether you think you can or you can't, you're right." A lot of it is up to you whether you're going to get something accomplished. If you think you can't do it, you won't. But if you think you can, you have a fighting chance. If you look at every obstacle in a positive light and dream about what will happen if you do succeed, then you have an opportunity to accomplish something.

It has been my mission in life to "get off my knees." To me that means hard work, independent living, and being a productive person in society, a taxpaying citizen, and, most important, a good family person. It also means you don't spend time complaining about things you can't control and you don't look for what's wrong—you look for what's right!

8

First Impressions

THERE ARE A FEW THINGS I've come to accept regarding my physical disability: (1) I'm never again going to ride a roller coaster (once is enough), (2) I'll never be taller than my children again, and (3) I'm going to make quite a first impression on people. In the latter case, I will do everything in my power to make you forget this initial impression. You see, the most important skill I've acquired as a person with a disability is that I am keenly aware of my first impression and how it might affect others.

Generally, that first impression of me is one of shock, awe, or surprise, and that's not what I want people to remember. I want them to remember me for the person I am on the inside, not just what they see on the outside. It's not easy to do, especially in the sales world, where first impressions are everything. But if I can get a potential client to put aside what I look like and at least think about who I am on the inside (educated, responsible, hardworking, funny, very knowledgeable about the TV industry), it's ultimately to their benefit.

I have spent a lifetime trying to overcome and block out people's first impressions of me, but there have been some memorable failures. In 1998 I flew to Norfolk, Virginia, to interview for a sales job with the NBC affiliate there. The sales manager was to pick me up at the airport, but he had no idea what I looked like, other than that I was wearing a shirt and tie. I chose not to reveal my physical disability to him beforehand because I didn't think I had to; after all, would someone who is African American be expected to tell a potential employer she is black?

When I arrived at the airport, the guy walked right past me. I knew it was him, and I was certain he knew who I was because we were the only two people at the airport dressed for business. I chased him down and said, "Are you looking for John Robinson? I'm John." He immediately did a double take. There was an uncomfortable silence, and I could see that he was embarrassed. The interview might as well have ended right there, because I could tell by his reaction he was uncomfortable with me, and I didn't want to work with someone who was more concerned with how I looked than whether I was a good salesperson.

I did learn a few valuable lessons from this experience, however. From that point on, I made sure to tell people in advance about my outward appearance, even though I didn't think it was necessary or appropriate. The experience taught me that I should be comfortable enough to say, "Hey, I am physically disabled, and you should know it." Invariably, what happens is the potential employer or client says it doesn't matter, but whether it does or it does not, at least they know. It shouldn't be important, but to an older generation that may be less accepting or educated about these physical differences, it might be.

That point brings me to the second lesson, which is that it's my responsibility to come prepared for whatever reaction people have toward me. If I can sense they're uneasy, I've got to do my best in those first few minutes to make them feel more comfortable. The unfortunate part about the Norfolk experience was that I wasn't concerned at all about first impressions or what I'd say during the interview process. I was supremely confident I could do the job. I was more worried about getting on and off the plane, how I was going to carry my bag, and whether I could find a suitable bathroom to use at the airport. It never crossed my mind that the sales manager might have a problem with my appearance. I wasn't ready for that kind of response, nor was I capable of defusing the situation.

It's not easy to make people forget their first impression of you when you stand less than four feet tall and they can't see you when you're standing on the other side of their desk. To overcome that obstacle, I try to get them to talk about themselves as quickly as possible, which shifts the attention away from me. I might try to interject a little humor or find some common ground with that person. For example, if I see that he has a Syracuse diploma on his wall, I'll find out right away if he is a sports fan and get his take on the Orange's new football coach or their most recent basketball game. Maybe she has a Cleveland Browns banner on her wall, in which case I'll make sure to poke fun at her for my Pittsburgh Steelers' most recent demolition of her team. What you can't do is have a negative reaction or no reaction at all, because it will just make the person feel even more uncomfortable.

In the sales world, you have to put the client at ease, and humor is one way to break the ice and get the client to engage you in conversation. Usually, people are so surprised by how I look that they immediately let their guard down and become more curious about me. Once I get them interested in me, then I have the opening I need to start talking about them and what their needs are.

There are two kinds of reactions I see when people first get a look at me: either they're surprised and embarrassed and just want to get on with business, or they smile right through, at which point we both can laugh a little bit. I have to read people and see how uncomfortable they are with their initial reaction toward me. One thing that has helped is my interaction with kids. When kids meet me, they have the most unfiltered reactions: "Why do you look so funny?" "Why are you so short?" "Where are your hands?" They will say anything, whereas their parents will bite their tongues. They'll think it, but they've been taught not to say it. I've had kids embarrass their parents to the point that they pull them away from me or, even worse, scream at them! I immediately tell the parents it's okay. Kids see eye to eye with me, so they can't understand why their parents would get angry at them. Their reactions are normal and honest, and they probably reflect the same response adults have toward me. Let's face it, when a child sees me in the grocery store and says, "See, that guy has no hands," they are right.

So as I've learned how to deal with children, it's helped me better manage my first impressions with adults. I answer the kids' questions, make light of the fact that I am different, and try to be as positive as possible. It's the same thing I do with adults. That doesn't mean I'm always perfect. My wife, Andrea, likes to remind me that in one very angry moment I said to an especially obnoxious child, "It's because I didn't eat my vegetables." That one had the child's parents laughing while he cringed. It was one of my better jokes, but it's one that I try to keep under wraps now.

Once I get beyond the initial first impression, I still have to make a sale. I have to sell my abilities to the potential employer or client and convince them that I do have something to offer their business. As I previously mentioned, before I got my first sales job with WSTM-NBC3 in Syracuse in 1994, I interviewed with about twenty other stations. I had the degree and the know-how to get any one of those jobs, but I didn't have enough job experience for it to be the tipping point. They could all cite my lack of experience for not hiring me, although I'm sure if I were able-bodied I would have landed one of them.

Eventually, what it came down to at WSTM is that I really wanted to sell for them and I found somebody I could connect with, someone who looked beyond my appearance and bought into the fact that I was a viable candidate. Still, even after I told the sales manager I'd work for the station at 100 percent commission, he had to convince his boss that I was someone worthy of hiring.

His boss's chief concern was, "How do we fire this guy if it doesn't work out?" Fortunately, they gambled on me.

I had all of the things they needed in a salesperson: I was eager to work, I was willing to make sales calls, I was memorable (more on that subject later), and I could talk about television as a product. During the interview the sales manager who hired me, Bob Eckel, said, "Sell me this coffee mug." Instead of saying, "Here's a mug— it's white and it's durable," I said, "Here's something that will get your morning off to a great start." It was exactly what he wanted to hear because he didn't want me selling the mug; he wanted me selling the coffee that was in the mug. That's what all owners want: They advertise with you because they want more patrons to walk into their stores or places of business. They don't care so much about the actual advertisement as they do the number of people who see it.

I was willing to accept WSTM's offer of a 100 percent commission job with no existing accounts because I believed in myself enough that if someone was willing to take a chance on me, I'd take a chance on them. Sometimes you have to make some concessions in order to get what you want; the payoff will come later. It's all about looking at obstacles as opportunities. Put yourself in the shoes of the employer and ask yourself, "Why do I take a chance on you?" In today's economic climate, there are a lot of people looking for work and not a lot of jobs to be had. The demand far outweighs the supply. If you're physically disabled, the odds are stacked even more heavily against you. *Seventy* percent of all people with disabilities are unemployed!

If you're one of these 70 percent or you're part of the growing national unemployment rate, keep plugging away. If you get an interview, make the best first impression possible under the circumstances. Don't walk in there with a defeatist attitude or a "the world owes you" attitude. Tell them what you have to offer and why you can make a difference for them. If you're a wounded veteran coming back from Iraq without an arm or leg, you need to think about what you have to offer society, not what you can't do. You have the kind of technical training and discipline that few other people have; you matter to some employer. Conveying that idea to the person sitting across the table or desk from you is all that really matters. It's how you get someone to forget that awkward first impression.

Of course, for a person with a disability, the first impression can work either for or against you. I said earlier that one advantage to being as short and funny looking as I am is that I am memorable. People are always going to remember me for how I look. And in my business, where first impressions are critical, that fact is a huge plus. There's a reason pharmaceutical companies hire young, attractive people (mostly women) in sales: they want you to remember who's selling. If a TV station has a sales staff of eight people, you can bet at least two of them will turn a few heads. It's part of the world we live in.

Look at some of the advertisements you see on television. You've got these local car dealerships screaming into your sets, trying to set themselves apart from their competition with the loudest, most outrageous promotion they can come up with. Why? Because it's memorable! Readers in the New York metropolitan area probably remember those Crazy Eddie electronic-store ads from the 1970s and '80s with the frenetic lead character screaming, "His prices are *insane!*" Those ads were widely popular and helped the chain earn more than three hundred million dollars in sales.

The television industry is no different from the real world: we're all trying to stand out and be noticed. If you're dating someone new, what do you do? You wear your best clothes, look nice, and try to smell good. It's your way of marketing your best qualities by highlighting your differences. In the sales world, my physical disability is what allows me to set myself apart from my peers. My disability is louder than any commercial or gimmick. But once I have the recognition, I still must provide substance. Just like the attractive salesperson with the million-dollar smile, I've got to be able to back it up. I can't just go in there looking the way I do and say, "Listen to me." I have to say, "I'm John Robinson. I'm here to talk to you about something specific to your business, and here's why you need to listen to me. I can help grow your business. I can drive traffic to your store. I can enhance your image in the community."

I have to produce that much more, because as the earlier example from Norfolk shows, being memorable isn't always a one-way ticket to the promised land. Whether you're a person with a disability like me or a war veteran, burn victim, or short in stature, that first impression is something you have to nail. It can be an opportunity for you, but only if you're keenly aware of how that first encounter may affect other people and you are prepared to show them that you're much more than just what they see on the outside, or on a piece of paper. Find out what it is you have to offer them, whether it's a job you're seeking or a relationship you're trying to further along, and like the maniac in the Crazy Eddie commercials, be passionate about it.

9

Listening Is Learning

MY BOSS at WSTM-NBC3 in Syracuse, Bob Eckel, used to say to me, "John, you should have stayed in the family business." He said I had a gift for talking, listening, and empathizing with whatever the situation was, all characteristics of a good priest. And a good salesperson.

It helps to be memorable and good looking, but the best salespeople are the ones who take the time to *listen* to their client's problems before they ultimately solve them. No matter what it is you're selling—computer software, color copiers, or a thirty-second spot on your local NBC affiliate—at the end of the day, you're trying to make your client's business better. In television, it means bringing more eyeballs to their business so they can increase sales. They're not buying an advertisement so much as they are buying the number of people who see that ad, because it's how they'll grow their business. Whatever problem, hurdle, or impediment is in their way, it's my job to listen first and then come up with an affordable solution to free up their time and increase their profits.

Over time, I've learned to become an excellent listener, partly due to my physical disability but also because I had some good mentors in my family who practiced this discipline every day. My maternal grandfather, Jacob Burge Morris, was not a very verbose person, but he made it a point to listen to the surroundings as much as he did other people. I remember one particularly hot and humid summer day at my grandparents' farm, a perfect day for a thunderstorm. My grandfather was bailing hay on one of the larger fields and, sensing that a storm might be brewing, summoned my uncle home from work to help him rake the hay. My grandmother took out a third tractor to load the wagons into the barn. I knew it was a major event, but I wasn't sure why until I noticed the sky. To the west, it turned black and turbulent. I knew then why there was so much activity: my grandfather had "listened" to the day and moved to finish the work ahead of the weather. The storm produced a lot of rain, but the hay was saved.

The other thing I learned (and it has taken a long time to learn) from my grandfather that has served me well in my career is patience. He read other people very well, and knew how to deal with certain situations with relative calm. There were no peaks or valleys with him; he always kept his emotions in the middle. He never got too animated or upset. By observing him and how he dealt with other people, I realized that you gain nothing by getting all worked up over a problem; it's better to exercise patience and then use your best judgment.

My father is another kind of listener. The stereotype of a priest is of a preacher at the pulpit, but the majority of my dad's time was spent listening to the problems of the members of his parish. His job was to balance the needs of many while listening to the problems of all. In essence, he was everyone's counselor. It meant being on call twenty-four hours a day, seven days a week. I can remember watching movies as a child and pausing them because someone was calling my dad, seeking his advice. The phone calls never ceased, whether it was someone dealing with a sick relative, depression, pregnancy, an abusive situation, a child in need, work-related stress, and so on. Fairly late one evening someone called my dad because he was upset over his son's playing a video game that concluded with the son killing the father (probably one of the *Star Wars* games, when I think about it).

The thing about my dad that I really came to respect is that he took every call and never complained about them. He taught me how to listen, sure, but he also showed me through his selfless actions how to best deal with problems: head-on. You may have a client who's giving you headaches, but the sooner you deal with him, the better the situation will become.

It's not easy to offer suggestions to anyone who has a problem. You may think you have the answer, but it's always better to lay back and let the client work through the problem and come up with her own solution. You listen and offer subtle advice; you don't force the solution on her, which is another thing I learned from my father, the priest. He would get a phone call from a parishioner with a family problem and spend most of the call listening to what was being said, not forcing his opinions. Had my mother been in that position, she would have been bolder and quicker to express her opinion. It was my father I watched to see how he listened and healed.

In sales, the best close to a deal is silence. The less you have to talk, the better; you let the client tell you when he is ready or not ready to suggest a solution. Most people have the solutions to their problems; they just have to work themselves through them. This fact holds true in business and in everyday life. I wish I had known it earlier in my life because in those times when I have been forceful with my opinion, or my personality, I have almost always had negative results. I'll use my oldest son, Haydon, as an example. He was a very hyperactive kid, so we tried to impose more discipline on him when what he probably needed was for his parents to lay back and let him vent his energy. We've been much easier on our other two children. There were also times early in my career when I failed to get promoted that I let my feelings be known, when what I should have been doing was listening to why they were promoting someone else over me. Looking back now, I see I still had much to learn. But I didn't want to hear it at the time.

The other gift my father has is the ability to convey how much he cares. It has made him a good priest. He took every call, visited anyone who was sick, and interrupted his day off on a weekly basis just to make that other person feel important. Doing so was at his own expense. My father still receives calls from parishioners in churches he led twenty years ago. He made them feel special. He listened and empathized with their problems. I hope to build those kinds of relationships.

If you need someone to hear your problems, a priest is a natural choice; a television account executive is not.

But my physical disability has made me into a good listener. While my high school friends were off playing soccer or basketball, I was in the stands, listening to girls' problems. Why? Because I was no physical threat to them. I wasn't going to take advantage of them, and they were not going to fall in love with me and get hurt. It didn't take me long to realize that my best attribute—the way to get people to talk to me—is to listen to what people have to say. I was using my physical disability to my advantage, as an opportunity to learn about people through listening.

In high school I was privy to all sorts of boy problems, scholastic tragedies, and sibling issues I never had hanging around the guys. The girls found it much easier to talk to me than to their parents about their problems because of how I looked, and because we were the same age. It was a blessing, because it allowed me to make friends, and a curse as well. It wasn't much fun hearing about the boys that my friends liked, because they were expressing their interest in them and not me. But I learned not to take what was confided in me personally. I had to give advice based solely on my opinion.

This nonthreatening front gives most people the opening to start telling me their problems. When I meet with a potential client for the first time, I don't have to work as hard as most other salesmen do. When the client sees that I am different, they're curious to know more about me, so they start asking me questions. It gives me the opportunity to ask questions and learn about them, and it isn't long before I have a good understanding of what it is they need for their business. That's a huge advantage for me. It's the same advantage a good-looking salesperson has, because the client is going to take an interest in her. If I were just a normal-looking guy walking in off the street, they wouldn't be as curious about me, and it would be much tougher to get them talking. A good salesperson will do whatever she can to get a client talking.

The other big advantage that my physical disability affords me is that I'm accustomed to facing difficult challenges and finding solutions to them. I had to learn how to drive a car, button my shirt, change a diaper with no hands, and prepare in advance for situations where I couldn't rely on other people's help to knot my tie or reach a household appliance. What was an afterthought for most people required much study and diligence from me. I had to be observant and smart—something that my grandfather taught me. I used my brain a lot when I was young because I wasn't trying to become the star quarterback or chasing girls. I studied people and I read history. I may not have had the physical strength, but I could think my way through a problem. Today, I can have a conversation with almost anyone and not be embarrassed by what I know or don't know.

However, if I can't solve a client's problem, I will tell him. I won't do something that's wrong for him in the long run, because if I say I can solve his problem and can't, he'll never forget it. If a client came to me today and needed help boosting sales of her women's fragrance, I'm going to politely turn her away. Our PBS station provides kids' programming during the day and reaches a fifty-plus audience at night, so we're not going to be any help reaching her targeted demographic, which is probably young women from ages eighteen to thirty-four.

The ability to listen and solve problems is the core of who I am today. My friends, peers, and clients seek out my attention to their problems. I have had clients from my WSTM days in Syracuse contact me in Albany for recommendations on their business marketing plans. When I was at WNYT-NBC13, other salespeople came to me for advice with issues related to sales. I guess they trusted my opinion, or felt that I understood them better because of the problems I've had to overcome in my life. Whatever it was, having people with twice my sales experience coming to me for advice was very flattering.

My sales managers did not like that other salespeople came to me and not them for advice—it was something that frequently came up in my reviews—but I cannot make myself less approachable. And I don't want to; if it ever comes to the point that I do not care about listening to and helping others, then I have stopped being a salesperson of any value. I would cease to be a person of any value if I did not care about the people around me. People enjoy talking to me because I take the time to listen, and I care about them.

Nothing bad comes from listening. You can always find some commonality with another person to have a conversation, which comes through listening and observing. The journalist who is conducting research for a story is "listening" to what she is reading, so she knows what questions to ask; the salesperson at your local Ford dealership is observing you the minute you walk onto the lot to see what catches your eye and what doesn't, so he is better prepared to make a sale.

The biggest challenge for many people with disabilities like myself is to get people to listen to them, yet a lot of that burden falls on us, too. Many people with disabilities shut down and don't want to deal with other people. It's much easier not to, especially in this computer age. But you've got to force yourself to try. Listen to what the world around you is telling you. It may be difficult to hear, but you have to listen to it. Doing so makes you better prepared to deal with it. Yes, I wish society looked at me differently, but I can't control its perceptions. What I can control is how I act and interact with other members of society. Only then can I get people to see me differently.

10

How to Deal
with Rejection

UNLESS YOU HAVE a very thick skin, it can be hard to
stay excited about selling. There is constant rejection. It
is the very nature of sales. There are thousands of sales
trainers—that is, counselors—needed to help you stay
focused on the goals ahead and keep you from choosing
another field.

There is a very diverse skill set that is required to
be an effective salesperson. You need to be able to com-
municate effectively, gain the trust of the people around
you (clients as well as peers), and let rejection teach and
motivate you. And you must be able to do it day after day
after day. You are only as good as your last day, week, or
month of sales. I had a sales manager, Bob Eckel, once
tell me that the highs are great and the lows are hard, but
you have to find the middle ground. Selling for a living
is a roller coaster. We all have to find our way back up
on that roller coaster and take a breath before the rise or
plummet.

Attitude is important in climbing out of any low,
which is as true in life as it is in sales. In both, it's the

people who realize there are ups and downs that are able to adjust better. They use a positive attitude to affect the world around them, instead of the other way around. When people allow hard times to affect them in the long term, then depression sets in. It can be difficult to climb out of a depressed state.

One of my greatest gifts is my attitude. I have never been one to sit at home and feel sorry for myself. I do not dwell on poor experiences from the past; rather, I look toward the future with hope. I look to the next opportunity, birthday, and experience as a challenge. It took me four years and countless interviews to land a job in television after graduating from college, but I did not view each rejection as a failure or a reflection on me and what I thought I was capable of doing. I brushed them off as best I could and looked forward to the next interview.

Rejection is something we all have to deal with; some, like myself, much more so than others. As a teenager I wasn't the image of what a girl was looking for in a boy. I wasn't cute, I wasn't strong, and I couldn't throw a football fifty yards or run down a quarterback behind the line of scrimmage. Successes for me were the little things, like making friends, getting an education, and learning how to dress and drive a car. It was about being accepted. The successes I think about today are the ones that came much later in life. Early on, I was careful not to put myself in positions where I could be turned away. I didn't try out for the wrestling team or the basketball squad, although I did once briefly flirt with the idea of joining the lacrosse team because no one in my high school really knew how to play. I had been tossing a ball around for years. But ultimately, I chose not to put myself out there.

Eventually, I learned that I wasn't going to get anywhere in life and stand on my own if I was afraid of failing. A few years after graduating from Syracuse I moved to Toronto to take a job with a telemarketing training company. I was asked to attend an outing at a local amusement park. I had been turned down for so many positions since college that I didn't feel like I was in a position to say no.

Theme parks have never been my most favorite places in the world to hang out, but I said I would go. On the day in question, we all went to Canada's Wonderland, with more than two hundred attractions, sixty-five rides, and some of the largest roller coasters in North America. I hated heights as well as fast movement, so the idea of riding a roller coaster was extremely disconcerting to me. But I figured I'd be off the hook, since most of the modern-day roller coasters would allow only people of a certain height, usually four feet, to ride. I was three-foot-nine. This thought put me somewhat at ease. Unfortunately, there was this one old wooden roller coaster at the park that allowed people three and a half feet or taller to ride—presumably younger children with their parents. My new colleagues urged me to join them on this roller coaster, and I obliged. What a mistake!

Unlike the newer roller coasters that had a shoulder harness and a seat belt, this coaster had the old-fashioned metal bar that would come down over your legs. I sat in the cart with my new boss, who was only two years older than I was, and before I could change my mind and escape we were climbing the first hill. The metal bar came down over his lap nice and snug, and he grabbed the bar with his hand. I was unable to grab the bar. So I bent myself over the bar and held onto it the best I could. It was bad. As we reached the top of the first hill and the car started to hurtle toward the bottom, I found it too difficult to hold on. We hit the bottom and rounded the first corner very hard, and as I turned and looked at my boss in the seat next to me I said, "I'll see you later," as in, I'm a goner! He knew exactly what I meant, and just as I started to lose all contact with the car he grabbed me and threw me down onto the floor. He saved my life for sure.

If I hadn't felt the need to involve myself in that ice-breaking exercise at Canada's Wonderland, I would've never put myself in a position to be on a roller coaster, clinging for my life. If I hadn't been rejected so many times, I would've had more confidence to say no in that situation. And therein lies the funny thing about rejection: it taps the reservoir of self-confidence that you have, yet, as I learned from that day forward, it also motivates you like nothing else. You learn how to bounce back, and from it you gain self-confidence. In sales you have to put yourself in a position to be rejected or accepted, usually in that order. You are unsuccessful far more times than you are successful, but a good salesperson learns to put the negatives behind them and focus on the successes. You learn not to take your rejections personally and move on. It's the same in life: if you interview for a job and don't get it, or you get rejected by someone you asked out on a date, you can't let it beat you up; you have to believe there is something better for you down the road.

I remember a job interview with two local sales managers at a different Syracuse TV station prior to my hiring at WSTM-NBC3. The two men asked me a series of questions to see if I was "ready." They wanted to know how I would sell—my sales background—and whom I would reach out to if I was hired. I mentioned I would call any business that I could think of; I had years of telemarketing experience and understood that the more calls you make, the more chances you have at being successful. One of the managers then asked whom I specifically knew in the Syracuse market. Could I name the general managers of the businesses along Erie Boulevard, a popular stretch of road for car dealerships, restaurants, and stores in the city? How could I possibly know? How could someone who had just moved to a new city with years of telemarketing experience in a different country know the names of the players in the new market? After leaving the interview, I realized that I had been set up to fail. I found out later that one of the sales managers wanted to hire me and one did not. It was the one who did not who asked me that question.

I was angry, certainly, but I didn't let it deter me from interviewing for the next TV sales job that came along. And that one—WSTM—just so happened to give me my big break and hire me. Part of the reason I was so persistent in my quest to land a TV sales job was my background in telemarketing. It started in high school in Manchester, where I sold carpet-cleaning appointments out of someone's basement one summer and vinyl siding the next. In telemarketing, you become accustomed to hearing the word *no*. But I didn't mind it so much because, for the first time in my life, people weren't saying no to my physical appearance; they just didn't want the product I was selling. I could handle it, and I used it to my advantage: I wasn't easily discouraged from picking up the phone and making the next call.

My second job in Toronto was also a telemarketing job, selling advertising for specialty trade publications throughout the United States and Canada. It was a 100 percent commission sales job, and it was my responsibility to make fifty phone calls per day to find potential ads. I was willing to make the calls that other people didn't want to make, so I got pretty good at it. For every fifty calls I made, I produced about three sales on average. That proportion is an awful closing ratio for most businesses, but for an inside sales job it was pretty good, and it was wonderful training. I learned persistence and patience. If the person on the other end of the line said "maybe" they were interested, I would not quit until I had an answer one way or another. Most sales trainers will tell you that the word *maybe* is a cover for *no*, but when *yes* is so seldom heard, *maybe* means *keep trying*.

Every phone call in sales has the same probability of being successful; you just don't know when the next success is coming. And that's why you keep picking up the phone and dialing. The two people responsible for hiring me in Toronto, Robert Thompson and Jack Smith, taught me this fact. I owe them so much for the opportunity to learn how to sell advertising. I had a college degree in television, radio, and film management, but it took two sales managers in publishing to teach me how to sell.

When I landed at WSTM in Syracuse, I was able to apply what I learned in Toronto to TV sales. But my education wasn't done. While Mr. Thompson and Mr. Smith taught me about persistence and perseverance, Bob Eckel showed me how to remain even-keeled in the up-and-down world of sales. "If you make a big sale, that's great, but you've still got to go to work tomorrow," he said. "And if you fail, that's fine. You stay in the boat, and you keep paddling."

He also advised me not to dwell on the negatives, or failures, and to focus only on my successes. The good news is there were more positive results in TV sales than in telemarketing, but I was still unsuccessful more often than not. I would make a sale about 35 to 40 percent of the time, which, being a stat guy, I likened to hitting about .350 in the major leagues. You hit .350 in the big leagues, and you've probably got yourself a batting title. A baseball player who hits .333 in the majors is considered a great hitter, and probably an all-star, yet he's successful only one-third of the time. In the advertising world, a batting average of 35 to 40 percent is excellent. And the more I sold, the more confidence I gained and the less I thought about the other 60 to 65 percent of the time when I struck out.

I don't think it's great advice to tell someone to learn from their mistakes. I think you learn more by what you do right. Six months after I was hired at WSTM, Bob and I went on a sales call together to pitch an idea I had for a computer software company to be a local sponsor for the upcoming 1996 Olympic Games. We would tout them as a gold-medal business and give them a platform to showcase their product, team, and the way they do things. Fifteen years later it's still the only time in my career that I've had someone write me a check for fifteen thousand dollars on our first meeting. Bob was certainly impressed, but what I got out of it is if you have a strong idea and you're passionate about what it is you're selling, then you have a good chance at being successful.

It takes practice, so when you experience success at something, ask yourself what it is you did right, why it came out right, and how you can emulate it the next time. Whatever you did right, think about it and work it through to the next stage. The more you concentrate on what you did wrong, the more likely you are to repeat that failure. Think about it: If you're coaching a poor free-throw shooter, you don't say to him, "Okay, your percentage stinks, so go practice your free throws." Instead, you say, "Okay, here's what you did really well on that last made free throw, so now go work on it."

Rejection has been as much a part of my personal life as it has my business career. I've been passed over for numerous jobs and promotions when I was clearly the more qualified candidate, but these losses came much later in my life when I was better equipped to handle them. When I was a child, it was much more difficult to accept.

I played T-ball growing up in Greene with some measure of success. I could hit the ball, whether it was pitched to me or placed on a tee, and I had figured out a way to transfer the ball from my glove to my right arm and fling the ball to first base. But when it came time to sign up for Little League, I learned I wasn't wanted. I don't know if it was because the bases were farther away and they figured I'd have trouble running them or because they just didn't want to accommodate me, but I wasn't allowed to play. I was devastated. In today's society, I would have been accommodated and allowed to play, because I would have been viewed as an inspiration to the other kids and a symbol of good sportsmanship. But in the 1970s in small-town USA, people were used to throwing things in the closet and forgetting about them. My parents were asked not to have me play.

Whether consciously or not, I used that rejection as a reason to learn how to play golf. I loved baseball as a kid, but golf provided me with a means to play against others on a level playing field. And I could play alone, too, if I so desired. It's a game with a scoring system ironically named for a disability (a "handicap" system) that allows me to play.

The dating situation for me wasn't quite as fair. My wife, Andrea, is not the first person I dated, and certainly not the first person I tried to date. I remember asking out a woman I worked with in the summer during college. I was persistent and continued to ask her out until she said yes. She didn't know me very well other than the fact that we worked together. I would have been better off asking a friend from school, but I didn't.

I took her to the movies on our date and offered to buy her coffee afterward. During the whole movie she was shaking and looking around to see if anyone noticed us together. Needless to say, it was a bad date. I had to make sure my self-confidence was in the right place and my next date was interested in who I was on the inside before I'd go out and be humiliated again.

I could never understand why girls didn't like me. In one particularly frustrating situation, I asked the daughter of a family friend out on a date. She refused. My father later explained to me that I'd be okay in the long run if I presented a happy, stable, and supportive picture. I may not have a lot of success early on, he said, but I can be a good husband and father. He was right. It wasn't much help at the time when I wanted to be a normal teenage boy dating other teenage girls, but I realized in college and later on that I did have a lot to offer someone.

Just as I had to learn how to be a friend to others, I had to learn how to be a friend to myself. I needed to do both of those things before I could find someone interested in dating me. It put me behind as far as learning "the moves." There were people interested in me, but I needed to make sure it was for the right reasons. I missed some signals early on in college by a few girls who did like me. One young woman came to visit me in my dorm room every day before and after dinner, and we'd talk. I had no idea she was interested in me. But over time I realized that my earlier rejections had painted a picture of what I was looking for in a mate.

Part of being a person with a disability is learning your way through life's obstacles through trial and error. And dating is no different. As in sales, I was unsuccessful much more than I was successful, but I never stopped trying. I had a choice to make in life. I could have decided early on to sit on a couch and collect whatever Social Security the government allowed. It would have been an easier but less gratifying life to take taxpayers' money instead of becoming a taxpaying citizen. I am proud I have pushed myself. If I had been depressed about my situation and abilities, my choice would have been different. It is my outlook on life that made the difference. I wish everyone could have my outlook on life and use it for themselves.

Keep paddling.

11

FAMILY MAN

IT WAS INEVITABLE. The family gathered upstairs in the laundry room where, on the wall, pencil markings recorded the steady growth of our three children: Haydon, Ariel, and Owen. Owen, the youngest at five years old, stood with his back to the wall to be measured. My wife, Andrea, took out a pencil, ordered Owen to stand nice and tall—which he had little trouble doing—and drew a firm line on the wall at the top of his head. Sure enough, he had eclipsed the high mark of his daddy, all three feet nine inches of him. I was now the shortest person in our immediate family, a distinction I will hold for the rest of my life.

Owen left the room cheering wildly, as if he had been told we were going to McDonald's for lunch. It's always an exciting moment for the kids when, around their fifth or sixth birthday, they realize they're taller than their father. It doesn't happen in most households when the children are five years old. Many kids never grow up to be taller than their fathers. But in our household, it's almost like a passing of the torch. I'm okay with it. I came to grips years ago with the reality that I'd one day be shorter than all of my children. Do I wish I were taller? Certainly. But you've got to be a father no matter what size you are, and it's more about their happiness at the moment than any loss I may be feeling.

I was thrilled for Owen.

I've been extremely fortunate to have three children who essentially could not care less how their father looks. To be honest, they think less about my physical disability than I do, largely because I'm the only dad they've ever known. They don't have another frame of reference, so they don't see what they may or may not be missing. They have adjusted to me just as I have to them. They understand they need to help me when I can't reach a bowl in the kitchen or a roll of paper towels at the supermarket, but they also expect me to feed them, read to them, and drive them to swimming and hockey practice. At that point, I'm very much a normal dad like anyone else.

I'm very proud of my kids and the way they've handled this difficult situation with such a positive and mature attitude. In many ways, it's a reaffirmation of what I've always believed with regard to seeing obstacles as opportunities. My kids see the glass as half full with me; they don't sulk or moan about what they don't have with me but focus on what they do have. When Haydon and I used to toss the football around, it was never, "Dad, I wish you could throw the ball ten yards farther." He was happy he had someone to throw the football around with.

Being a parent has given me the opportunity to look at myself and my disability with optimism. I realize that 95 percent of the time I'm just Dad. It's also taught me how to be better around other children. It wasn't always easy for me, but as soon as I became a parent to Haydon, I had to learn how to be more accepting of children's reactions. I vividly remember walking down Queen Street in Toronto with Haydon, then a two year old, and seeing other children pointing or staring at me, and in some cases even shouting at me. Their parents were often so embarrassed that they would drag their kids away and give them a good scolding in front of everyone. I wasn't always sure how to deal with this situation. Yet I knew that Haydon, as well as many of the other children, were watching me to see how I would handle it. I wouldn't be setting a very good example if I yelled back or made faces at the kids, so I decided to just go about my business and ignore them.

Kids are just curious, and, unlike most adults, their reactions are very unfiltered: they don't think about what they're going to say or how they're going to react; they just do it. And as the children saw me more and more around the neighborhood, they began to approach me, albeit hesitantly. In these instances, I used my disability to break the ice. I would touch the bump on my left arm, which my college buddies used to refer to as a "marshmallow," and simultaneously say, "Beep." Kids started to talk about the little man with the body part that sounded like a horn, and they would invariably become less frightened. I taught Haydon, Ariel, and Owen about the "beep." Over time, they could sense when a friend of theirs was uncomfortable with how I looked. They would walk up to me, invite the friend up to me, and say, "Look, he's okay—his marshmallow beeps!" It almost always works to ease the tension.

As my kids have gotten older, I have at different times asked them how my disability has affected them. Haydon, now in college, made the analogy that my dealing with my physical disability was like playing a video game for the first time on the expert level: it was extremely hard. It was his way of saying that he was very proud of me, because he understood the kind of physical and mental challenges I have had to confront every day of my life.

If anyone is more in tune to the way I'm feeling, and aware of my differences, it's Ariel. If someone stares or points at me, she'll come over to hug me or touch my arm. It's her way of checking that I'm okay. She's the most observant, caring, and sensitive of my kids, and it shows in her personality. To Owen, I'm still Dad. He doesn't care that I'm shorter than the next-door neighbor's father, not as long as I can talk about his favorite cartoon, discuss the Lego set he just built, or be there for him with a water bottle after his soccer game. The father Owen wants is the one who is there for him when he falls down and scrapes his knee. His friends may still point me out in the crowd as the short guy, but he doesn't care.

I have pushed myself really hard to be comfortable around my kids' friends. When Owen turned five I decided to volunteer as a coach for his soccer team. I never had the personal confidence in myself to coach Haydon's football or baseball team, or help with Ariel's swim team, but I figured that soccer for five year olds was something that I could tackle. I assisted another coach in teaching the twelve kids the fundamentals of soccer. It was much harder than I expected. I never ran so much in my life! The kids ran around and created havoc all over the field, without listening to anything I or the other coach had to say. I had no idea what I was doing. I was essentially a forty-year-old cheerleader. But the kids looked up to me. I was their coach because I was there for them; it's all they expected of me. They were very happy to have someone they could talk to at eye level. I realized over those three months that I could coach just as any parent could.

Although the idea of coaching one of my kid's teams wasn't very appealing to me early on, I did want to be involved in their schoolwork as much as I could. In 2002 I went to a parent-teacher meeting at Ariel's school, and her teacher asked for volunteers. I didn't know what I'd be volunteering for, but I said yes. It turned out that Mrs. Baldwin, Ariel's first-grade teacher, needed someone to come in every other week and help with reading. I could do it, I thought. I have never been comfortable in front of a large group of kids because they are usually more vocal in their surprise about my disability when in large numbers. But I didn't want to shy away from my responsibility of being Ariel's dad, and I thought it would be good for the twenty-five other first graders to see a person with a disability up there reading to them on a regular basis, so they could see that I was an ordinary person just like their parents. I'm happy I volunteered. I was received so well by the kids that I was asked by Mrs. Baldwin and the students to participate in a videotaped teleconference about the famous book *Where the Wild Things Are*. Over two years, they became very comfortable with me, and I with them. I was no longer terrified to be with a large group of kids. In many ways I think I got more out of volunteering those two years than the children did.

Of course, none of it would have been possible had I not found someone who was able to look beyond my outward appearance and believe in me as much as I believed in myself, someone who saw that I could be a good provider and a loving husband and father. I had hoped I could find someone with those qualities, but when I left for Toronto in June 1991, finding a wife and a mother to my future children was the furthest thing from my mind. I was all about work and building my career. And, for the first time in my life, I was truly standing on my own, trying to make ends meet.

I guess it's true what they say: love finds you when you're least looking for it, which is exactly what happened to me. On the very first day I moved to Toronto I met my future wife, Andrea. I had rented a room in a house with two actors, David and Mark, and Andrea lived next door. When I arrived, David was standing on the front porch smoking a cigarette with Andrea and her sister, Paige. I introduced myself to everyone there, not thinking for a minute that this particular moment would change everything.

The next morning while I was pulling out of the driveway for work, Andrea came out to see me. She had worked for several summers with disabled kids and was curious to know how I drove my car. As I was showing her the hand controls and explaining how I used them, it struck me how pretty she was standing there. But I didn't think I'd have the opportunity to be more than friends with her because I had learned the night before that she had a boyfriend and a two-year-old son, Haydon.

But we started to hang out together, and two weeks later I asked her if she wanted to go to a Toronto Blue Jays game. She agreed. I took the opportunity to let her drive my car, since she was in the process of getting her driver's license. It was one way I could return her kindness for welcoming me to the neighborhood. Over that summer we became very close friends. We'd sit on her front porch, have a beer or a cup of coffee, and watch the people go by on Queen Street. We'd also talk about my home in New Hampshire and other things, but I still didn't think that I had an opportunity to date her because of her boyfriend. As the summer wore on, however, it became more apparent to both of us that we really liked each other's company, and that we had something special going. She broke up with her boyfriend, and we were dating by August.

Had I met Andrea a few years earlier, I would have had no chance. I was shy in college and had very little experience with dating. So what happened? I discovered my strengths and used them to find happiness. When I was happy with myself, then I was able to project some confidence with women.

It began my senior year in college. I stopped dwelling on who I liked and started talking with those women who liked me. As a result, I tuned in more to what other people were feeling instead of being so self-absorbed. Doing so created a more giving personality, which was closer to my real personality. I became myself with women. What a change!

The more comfortable I became with myself, the more attractive I looked to other potential mates, friends, and clients. It took me a lot longer to learn this lesson than most able-bodied people, because I would always dwell on my disability. It was ironic that here was the one area of my personal life that I needed the most help, yet I couldn't see my own reality enough to help myself.

Andrea's parents, who lived only a few blocks away from her home in the Beaches section of Toronto, had barbecues just about every Sunday throughout the summer. All of Andrea's friends were welcome, including me, my roommate, David, and her roommate, Sonya. It gave me an opportunity to get to know them very well, and when Andrea announced that we were dating, they were very supportive. Andrea first met my parents in October and later in November at Thanksgiving. She, Haydon, and I made the trip up to New Hampshire together, and it was on the ride home that she revealed to me what she had told my friends that week: she could see herself marrying me someday. What she didn't know, however, was that I was thinking the same thing. I could not afford a large engagement ring at the time, so I purchased a ruby ring that weekend—a symbol of our future life together. We got engaged on that very car ride home to Toronto, at approximately two in the morning, no less.

We were married in June 1993, two years after I pulled up behind her house in Toronto. At the time of this writing, we are going on sixteen years of marriage. To many

22. In Montreal with my mother, Priscilla *(left)*, and my future wife, Andrea, in the fall of 1991. Andrea was meeting my parents for the first time on this trip.

people, the fact that I'm married is the most surprising detail about my life. I've had many friends tell me that when they reveal my story to other people for the first time, it's not my ability to play golf, drive a car, or manage a sales team that surprises them most but that I have been married for sixteen years and have three children. I'm not exactly sure why it's so surprising to them; perhaps it's because relationships are so very hard. We have many friends who are divorced. Andrea and I have had our shares of ups and downs, too, but we've been able to survive for the very same reasons we got together in the first place: because we like each other's company, and we don't demand so much of each other. Andrea lets me be who I am, and I do the same for her. I want her to go hiking because I know how important it is to her, and she understands my need to watch every single Boston Bruins game from October through May.

Several years ago I had the opportunity to speak to a group of mentally challenged people with disabilities. There were probably sixty people in the audience, which normally wouldn't have been such a big deal except that I had never spoken to a group of people with disabilities before. I was always speaking to the business community about my disability. I did not have a set speech prepared for this particular audience, and started out by talking about my parents and my education at Syracuse University. I said in passing that I was married with three children, and here was when I caught their interest. They had no commonality with a private school education or a priest father, but they all shared a love for their family and friends. When I indicated I was married, one couple interrupted me and said that they were together. The young man wanted me to meet his—in his mind—spouse. For the next half hour we went around the room and learned about the people whom everyone cared about most. There were stories about girlfriends and boyfriends, parents and siblings, which is how we connected.

It was the most gratifying evening I had talking about my disability. It reminded me of how I felt meeting Andrea for the first time, and how much I struggled to find someone I could spend time with. It once again

23. My wife, Andrea, and I sitting in our seats in section 211 at the Carrier Dome, Syracuse University. This photograph was taken by a gentleman who sat next to us at Syracuse football games for more than ten years.

verified for me that my struggle was inside my own mind. These developmentally challenged individuals had all the confidence in the world when it came to relationships, and for most of my life I had none. But at the time that I was speaking to them, that commonality was how they understood me. I learned more about relationships that evening than at any other single point in my life.

I take that knowledge with me every day in my sales career. It is the relationships and, more important, the ability to create relationships that set us apart from our peers. We can truly connect with one another once we are able to stand on the same level, when we believe in the other person as much as we believe in ourselves. This fact is true in any marriage, business relationship, or parenting situation.

There are many people with and without disabilities who wonder if they'll ever find true love and be able to have a family. They can, but they've got to be happy with themselves first. Both Andrea and I had this self-contentment in common when we first met. We were then able to display our best qualities to one another. If you always look at what's wrong with you, you'll project that negativity to other people. But if you focus on what you do like about yourself and concentrate on those things, then those things will be what you reflect to other people. Whether you're interviewing for a job, asking someone out on a date for the first time, or speaking in front of a group of fifty strangers, you should project a positive, happy image of yourself. Find out what you honestly like about yourself and what other people like about you, and use it to your advantage.

It's your way to "get off your knees" and stand up to the obstacles that are in front of you today, to be a happier and more productive person tomorrow.

Afterword

DAVE ALLEN

THE FIRST TIME I RECALL seeing John was in the first-floor gaming area in the lobby at Sadler Hall on Syracuse University's campus. He was wearing a Pittsburgh Steelers Bubby Brister jersey, number 6, and smoking a cigar. Very uncool, I thought. But those things were incidental observations. What I was really looking at were his arms and legs. "Where are they?" I thought to myself. Here was this little guy standing there, barely up to my waist, with no true arms or legs to speak of. I'm sure my reaction to John was the same everyone feels upon seeing him for the first time—a mixture of shock, amazement, fear, and curiosity.

That feeling of fear and curiosity stuck with me for several months my freshman year. I really didn't get to know John until deep into the second semester, partly because of that fear but mostly because our side of the hall on Sadler 1 didn't socialize with the other side too much. My side went out together and ate lunch together, and had it not been for intramural sports competitions, I'm not sure we would have ever gotten to know John. It also helped that I struck up a friendship with John's next-door neighbor Craig and that we all shared an interest in hockey. I was a New York Islanders fan, Craig a fan of the rival New York Rangers, and John of the Boston Bruins.

One Saturday late in the spring semester, we had a block party in Walnut Park along the campus's fraternity row. The Red Hot Chili Peppers were among the acts, and it was a rare sunny and warm day in Syracuse. After many beers I remember hanging out in John's room for the first time that night, talking about various things—mainly hockey and how much alcohol our bodies could tolerate—while nearly everyone else on the floor was passed out. From that moment on we forged a friendship that still goes strong today. In fact, I am the ghostwriter of this book, something I could never have imagined upon that first encounter in Sadler Hall nearly twenty-three years ago.

I am very lucky my curiosity won out. Our society, in general, does not take the opportunity to get to know people with disabilities. We marvel at them, we're easily inspired by them, and we empathize with them. But they remain, for the most part, strangers and, in most cases, outcasts to us all. What makes John such a remarkable person is that he never, for one minute, accepted it as his fate in life. He made a decision to stand on his own and become a productive member of our society, an integral part of which is being seen in public and putting himself out there to be rejected. He had to work hard at making friends. It didn't come easily with me, and it didn't come easily with a lot of the guys at Syracuse.

One of the guys who lived on my side of the floor freshman year at Syracuse was from Staten Island. Pat, John, myself, and a lot of the guys would watch the NFL games on Sunday in the common area in the lobby of Sadler 1. John was interested in getting to know Pat, but Pat was very reserved around John in the beginning and kept his distance. It troubled John, because it was symptomatic of the way a lot of people viewed him. Most of the people who talked to John did so out of curiosity, because he looked different, not because they had something in common with him or wanted to be his friend. John saw something in Pat—in this case, a common interest in sports, especially hockey—that he liked, and he wanted Pat to talk to him more. Eventually, once John stopped trying to impress people and realized he was better being himself around others, Pat became more accepting of him and they became good friends. They remain so today.

A lot of my closest friends outside of Syracuse and members of my family have met John and frequently ask how he's doing. He inspires everyone he meets, not so much because he drives a car, holds down a job, or breaks a hundred on the golf course, but because of his attitude toward life. He's never used his disability as an excuse for anything. That type of attitude has rubbed off on all of his friends because we'll be the first to tell you we don't cut him any slack. For anything. Every year I partner with John in a member-guest golf tournament outside of Syracuse at Camillus Country Club, and I get on his case if he hits a bad shot just as I would any able-bodied partner. If he three-putts from twelve feet, he's going to hear about it. Sometimes, even the other group gets into the act, and they might have known John for only a few hours.

Here is what is so remarkable about John: despite his physical differences, you become blind to them once you get to know him. You see a normal-looking person in front of you because he gives you no reason to believe he is different. He doesn't ask for special treatment on the golf course because he has no hands to hold the club. He makes no excuses if he loses his balance and tops the ball into the lake. He goes up there and does his best, and expects you to treat him just like anyone else when he mis-hits the ball, because after a while you don't feel like he's any more prone to making a mistake than you are.

In writing this book, I asked John who were his idols growing up, whom he had looked to for motivation during difficult times. He mentioned such athletes as Rocky Bleier, Thurman Munson, Lou Piniella, Joe Morris, and Steve Kasper. These individuals certainly weren't stars; they were either blue-collar guys or players who had overcome tremendous obstacles to make a name for themselves, such as Bleier, who had shrapnel removed from his thigh after being wounded in Vietnam. John rooted hard for these players because he was very much like them and could relate to the struggles they were enduring. They taught John that if you work hard enough, you can be a success no matter what obstacles stand in your way.

John is the one who inspires people today. I hope that from reading this book you'll gain the same level of motivation, confidence, and appreciation for life that I received writing it. No matter what your disability, problem, or personal struggle, you'll be much better prepared going forward having read this book. In today's tough economic times, with so much doom and gloom being reported in the news, we can always use a feel-good story. There are few stories about overcoming adversity that are better than this one.

I hope that, for those readers who are able-bodied, you'll gain a greater appreciation for people who are disabled or different after reading this book. By *different*, I'm referring not only to people with disabilities but to people of a different color, ethnicity, height, and so on. I hope you'll be more accepting of them, too, and that you'll act on your curiosity, as I and so many others did with John, and take the time to talk to them. You'll find that they feel the same things you do, are capable of loving the same way you are, and, if given the opportunity, can be productive members of our society. I still find it hard to believe—and unacceptable—that nearly 70 percent of all people with disabilities are unemployed. How many of these people would still be unemployed if given an opportunity to succeed? I bet not too many.

If there's anything that John has taught me over the years, it is to be more accepting of people with differences, whether they're physical or perceived. And he did it without saying a word about it. If I walk down the street and see someone in a wheelchair, or if I'm competing in a 10K race and one of the other runners has a prosthetic leg, I'm no longer shocked by what I see. Or surprised. If anything, I'm a little curious to learn about his or her story. *Get Off Your Knees: A Story of Faith, Courage, and Determination* is one such story, and one you'll be a much better person for having read.